Praise for *Reframe*

"*Reframe* is both a practical guide and a salve for the soul. It gives language to the unspoken truths many of us live with, explaining why we think and act as we do. For those of us who are Generalists, it shines a light on the often-invisible value we bring to the world and reminds us that we're not alone. Reading it gave me clarity about my own winding path and affirmed that the perspective we carry, while sometimes isolating, is exactly what's needed in times of change."

MIDY APONTE-VARGAS, President and Founder, Civil Strategies

"In a world of narrow career paths and siloed experience, Siobhán O'Riordan offers up a practical guide for the entrepreneurs, intrapreneurs, operational wizards, project leads, people managers, and leaders who bring expansive thinking, considered actions, and a desire to work across systems to solve entrenched problems."

GERALD CHERTAVIAN, Founder and Advisor, YearUp United and Senior Lecturer, Harvard Business School

"As a philanthropic futurist, I spend my days helping visionary leaders prepare for what's next. The pace of change isn't slowing down. The leaders who thrive will be the ones who can navigate volatility with creativity and range. *Reframe* is a practical and affirming blueprint for how to do just that."

TRISTA HARRIS, President of FutureGood and author of *Future Good*

"Being a Generalist in a Specialist's world is stressful. Most of us need to work to live, and that means we usually don't have the luxury of experimenting with our livelihood. There's an enormous amount of pressure—some self-imposed, but much of it very real—to "figure it out." I entered my career with few connections and minimal skills to self-advocate, so it took years of mentorship and trial and error to receive the kind of validation a book like this could have given me. It's comforting to know that you're not alone, and invaluable to hear that you have unique strengths that others don't."

CASSY KRUEGER, Organizational Effectiveness & Culture Designer

"Siobhán O'Riordan has written the book so many of us have been waiting for—especially those who've never quite fit neatly into one box. *Reframe* is like a permission slip for anyone who's ever felt like a 'jack-of-all-trades' but secretly wondered if that was a weakness. Siobhán flips that thinking on its head. She shows us that being a Generalist isn't just valid—it's powerful, necessary, and perfectly suited to the complex world we're navigating right now. If you've ever felt unseen or unsure how to articulate the value you bring, this book will feel like someone finally turned the light on."

JANINE GARNER, coach, speaker, podcast host, and author of *Be Brilliant* and *It's Who You Know*

"While the world celebrates specialists, Siobhán O'Riordan champions the questioners, connectors, and pattern-seekers who thrive in uncertainty and drive innovation. If you're tired of apologizing for your wide-ranging interests and ready to claim your role as an essential catalyst for change, this book will show you how."

OSCAR TRIMBOLI, award-winning podcast host and author of *How to Listen*

"At last, a guidebook to navigate a world that increasingly rewards specialization, but desperately needs the multi-faceted and multi-sectoral experience and wisdom of the generalist. Siobhán O'Riordan is the perfect guide for those of us who seek a broader path of contribution and change-making."

MICHELLE NUNN, President and CEO, CARE

"The world is changing dramatically—and so is the kind of leadership we need. In *Reframe*, Siobhán O'Riordan shows how Generalists—adaptive, curious, and action-oriented—can thrive in this new era. As a former CEO for thirty years and now a coach to dozens of CEOs, I've seen the power of both Specialists and Generalists. *Reframe* is an essential guide for leaders and employers alike, offering practical strategies and inspiring insights to unlock the full potential of Generalists."

VANESSA KIRSCH, Founder-in-Residence & Senior Partner at New Profit

"As an investor, advisor, and educator, I have spent my career cultivating future leaders in both the private and social sectors. I know first-hand that the pace of change isn't slowing down, and the ones who will thrive are those who can navigate volatility with creativity and range. *Reframe* equips the next generation of leaders with the mindset and tools to turn uncertainty into opportunity."

ARCHIE L. JONES, JR., Senior Lecturer, Harvard Business School and CEO of NxGen COACH Network™

"The rapid change in technology demands leaders who are adaptable and discerning, open to learning and growth. Siobhán's book *Reframe: How Generalists Thrive in a Changing World* gives systems builders, dot connectors, and those who fill in the gaps a guide to visioning and valuation to collaborate with leaders and specialists in new ways, and transform challenges into opportunities."

TINA HALFPENNY, CEO Efficiency Forward/Executive Director DLC

REFRAME

REFRAME

How Generalists Thrive
in a Changing World

SIOBHÁN A. O'RIORDAN

EAC
Books

Published by EAC Books, in partnership with Grammar Factory Publishing.

EAC Books and the EAC Books logo are trademarks of the Expert Author
Community (www.expertauthor.community), used under
license. Grammar Factory Publishing (www.grammarfactory.com)
is a registered trade name of MacMillan Company Limited.

MacMillan Company Limited
25 Telegram Mews, 39th Floor, Suite 3906
Toronto, Ontario, Canada
M5V 3Z1

O'Riordan, Siobhán A.
Reframe: How Generalists Thrive in a Changing World / Siobhán A.
O'Riordan.

Paperback ISBN 978-1-998528-48-6
eBook ISBN 978-1-998528-49-3

1. BUS012000 Business & Economics / Careers / General.
2. BUS060000 Business & Economics / Personal Success.
3. PSY036000 Psychology / Personality.

Production Credits
Cover design by Designerbility
Interior layout design by Setareh Ashrafologhalai
Book production and editorial services by Grammar Factory Publishing

CONTENTS

INTRODUCTION
UNSEEN AND UNSUNG

CHARISSE SAT WITH a former colleague over a Saturday coffee, regretting her career of false starts. Over the past fifteen years, her friends had built successful careers as lawyers and executives, with titles like "Director" and "Vice President." Charisse had just left her job after a year, again disappointed by working at another start-up where she failed to translate her early success into a permanent position. This happened a lot. She would join a company at the beginning and have immediate success in finding problems to solve. She had a knack for getting to know clients quickly and felt her "fresh eyes" gave her an advantage in finding ways to meet their changing needs. Yet, as each company soon grew, her once-exciting role of identifying and innovating solutions to meet client needs increasingly narrowed and focused on standardizing service. She soon became bored and frustrated as her job lost the creativity she had initially experienced and enjoyed. She knew being hired successively by so many companies was evidence of her intelligence and capability, and yet the many examples of her success were almost equal in number to the disappointments. Discouraged, she confided in her friend her doubts and the uncertainty of what to do next.

Or consider Nasir, whose personal story differed in several ways from the childhood experiences of his colleagues. His upbringing as a young immigrant navigating new environments provided him with a unique perspective as a consultant discerning client needs.

1

Nasir was valued by clients and colleagues alike for his ability to assess industries, quickly identify key opportunities to research, and make insightful and strategic recommendations. Quickly promoted to senior consultant, he was now pressured to focus on one industry. Nasir loved his job because he had constant exposure to new ideas and opportunities, including clients, industries, and challenges. The need to specialize in this new role robbed him of what he felt made him successful: the freedom to follow his curiosity, see patterns, and think broadly about solutions. Disappointed and discouraged, Nasir became convinced that consulting wasn't for him and soon left the company, landing a management role at a nonprofit organization.

And then there is Michelle, who, after university, followed in the footsteps of her trailblazer sister to work on cruise lines. With a new contract every four to six months, Michelle enjoyed her work, the places she traveled to, and the freedom to explore the world in between contracts. She loved everything about the life she had created, yet on curated social media posts and periodic trips home, she observed friends living a very different, even conventional, life. While they climbed the corporate ladder, got married, bought homes, and had families, she accumulated a list of countries visited and created unique memories through many once-in-a-lifetime experiences. Michelle questioned her unconventional choices after moving back to "land" permanently. The life led by so many people she knew and loved somehow did not work for her, and she was unsure what would.

ALL GENERALISTS,[1] INCLUDING Charisse, Nasir, and Michelle, experience what David Epstein describes in his book *Range: Why Generalists Triumph in a Specialized World*, as the "Generalist zigzag." When intentional, the "zigzag" is rewarding. Yet, for Charisse, Nasir, and Michelle, and many other Generalists, it is a byproduct of second-guessing choices and capabilities, wondering why they cannot do what others seem to do with ease: pick a lane, hone a skill, develop a career, climb the ladder. Instead, our need as Generalists for variability takes precedence. We thrive in roles that allow for our "ranging curiosity" and "creative approach" to problem-solving. When we default to what we think we should be, an expert, the attributes that make us successful in the right roles for Generalists fail us as Specialists. Our "ranging" curiosity lacks focus, our creative problem-solving is illogical, and our adaptability and experimentation are interpreted as lacking intention. This is what drives the cycles of confidence, curiosity, and success, followed by frustration, discouragement, and doubt for Charisse, Nasir, and Michelle, and so many other Generalists.

Even when we, as Generalists, find confidence, as Charisse, Nasir, and Michelle eventually do, we still struggle to communicate our value, understand our impact, or build a career because our work is largely unseen and unsung. Our "invisibility" begs the question: Why should we care about Generalists? And why now? This is one of the key questions I will answer in the pages that follow. But before I outline exactly what this book entails and how it can help you, I would like to introduce myself.

From one Generalist to another

My name is Siobhán O'Riordan. I am a Gallup®-Certified Clifton-Strengths® Coach with a BA in History and an MA in Teaching from Tufts University.

Before becoming a coach, I was a consultant and senior leader, working with and in organizations with revenues ranging from $500,000 to $30 million. I helped social entrepreneurs build their teams and create inclusive learning cultures. I scoped and implemented strategies to increase revenue, expand collaboration, and improve communication. I advised extensively on direction, programs, funding models, and messaging across all types of philanthropic organizations, including foundations and intermediaries.

At least that's what my bio says. But I also worked in public relations, taught high school history, catered, and sold antiques in addition to a slew of summer jobs. If you chart my career (and I do in Chapter 6), it is marked by highs that were both satisfying and award-recognized, followed by deeply discouraging lows. And yet I never understood this rollercoaster (zigzag!) of success and failure until seven years ago, when a colleague, Andrea McGrath, introduced me to the idea of a Generalist. Andrea described a Generalist as someone who is widely curious, often a quick study, ranges across careers, and finds success in any number of roles. I recognized myself immediately in her description, and, later, in David Epstein's book, *Range*. I welcomed having a word, even if undefined, that captured how I operate in the world.

Not unlike landing in a new environment without knowledge of the language, customs, or climate, until recently, being a Generalist lacked direction and was mostly "learn as you go." While I appreciated knowing there were others like me, that fact didn't answer the questions I had about how to *be* a Generalist in the world in which I live and work. And more specifically, how to understand and adequately explain my value, my strengths, and the kinds of conditions and challenges in which I thrive.

The book I needed, but didn't have

So, I set out to answer the question: What is a Generalist? In this book, I explore what we share and how we individualize; how we navigate our unique paths; and how we differ from, and yet very much need, Specialists. It was not just a definition or a description of what a Generalist is that mattered to me and the other Generalists I interviewed for this book. It was understanding why we struggle, where we excel, and how we can better deliver on our individual and collective value in a world that needs us to solve increasingly complex problems.

Five years ago, prompted again by a conversation with Andrea about the invisibility of being a Generalist, I wrote a popular post on LinkedIn.[2] Since then, I have coached and created a course for Generalists to help them handle role changes, handle new responsibilities as managers and leaders, and find new jobs. In every scenario, I helped each Generalist distill and define their narrative.

Who are they as Generalists? What is their unique value proposition and power? When and where do they find excellence? The answers are not obvious, and yet, like peeling an onion, we examine the layers of excellence and potential that have, for so many Generalists, been overlooked, ignored, and underutilized.

Witnessing my clients understand and embrace their version of a Generalist further inspired me to go deeper into the subject. I researched over 150 sources (including books, articles, videos, podcasts, and posts about Generalists), surveyed over 100 Generalists, and conducted twenty interviews. I had many more conversations with clients, other coaches, colleagues, and peers to inform the content of these pages. The research, my learning, and the challenges of our current moment all contributed to the content and influenced the layout, which is designed to encourage notes of your own.

This is the book I wish I had twenty-five years ago: a practical how-to guide for Generalists and professionals with multi-faceted careers, who are often lost in a world that rewards specialization. This is the book that could have helped me find clarity and confidence in my abilities as a Generalist, rather than failing to meet and being disappointed by imposed definitions of success.

The questions I ask and give guidance on in this book are the same questions my clients and other Generalists struggle with:

- What would happen if you, as a Generalist, could confidently communicate your value so others easily understand what you do?

- What would happen if every Generalist had the same kind of opportunities for growth, success, and development that Specialists have?

- What could collaboration with Specialists look like to help further shared success while building your own?

- What would it feel like if you could name your superpowers, carve a career you love, and have a vibrant network of other Generalists, all similarly unique?

- What could be possible if you and every Generalist could meet the unknown demands of the future?

If I have learned anything in my zigzag, roller coaster career, it is this: *the thinking that created the problem will not be the thinking that solves the problem.* Stubborn challenges and unpredictable change still require expert insights. Yet, increasingly, it will be new ideas and new approaches that meet the increasingly complex demands of our time. Demands that Generalists are uniquely positioned to address. This book provides Generalists with what they have long needed: a definition and framework within which to understand and communicate their unique value and create an aligned career. When Generalists can be and bring their best, Specialists can more easily do the same. It is only together that we can meet the demands of our rapidly changing world.

A practical guide for every Generalist at every stage

This book serves as a comprehensive and pragmatic guide for anyone who identifies as a Generalist at any stage in their career: an overview of the Generalist landscape, precise definitions, detailed descriptions, and relevant frameworks to support individual career development and direction. It is also a guide to navigating changing times and how to use our strengths, people skills, and values to make decisions with limited and imperfect information.

This book is intended to be a resource that Generalists can return to repeatedly as they seek first to discern their value and then develop their careers. (Managers, HR professionals, and others will also find the book relevant.) The layout of this book facilitates active reflection on the content with prompts, wider margins for note-taking, selected quotes for inspiration, and questions for further exploration. The workbook, accessed via the QR code, has additional exercises. The information shared invites individual consideration; not everything will apply to everyone. While a book for all Generalists, it is for you to make it your own. The case studies are anonymized and, in some instances, combined. However, all are drawn from real conversations with interviewees and coaching clients about Generalist challenges and successes.

The book is split into two parts. Part 1 consists of three chapters and provides definitions that Part 2 builds upon. Chapter 1 identifies the dilemma facing Generalists in being both unseen and increasingly in demand. In Chapter 2, we examine the broader context, types, and needs of Generalists to understand the challenges ahead better. Chapter 3 provides a framework and explanation of core Generalist attributes—curiosity, creative connections, and context—that Generalists can use to identify their areas of potential growth.

Part 2 has four chapters, exploring how we can understand, individualize, apply, and develop our value proposition as Generalists. Chapter 4 focuses on the power of understanding and discerning our strengths (not skills) in preparation for Chapter 5, which explores how to communicate and collaborate as a Generalist. Chapter 6 delves into key considerations when creating a career as a Generalist. Chapter 7 covers self-development and growth as a Generalist. The conclusion focuses on how Generalists can meet the needs of the future starting today.

We can no longer afford to leave Generalist talent on the table. To meet the unique demands of our time, Generalists need to receive the kind of support, visibility, and understanding that Specialists have long had. This book does precisely that by providing pragmatic and career-changing tools and tactics that elevate all Generalists, enabling us to see every single one of them.

1

THE GENERALIST'S DILEMMA

"In a wicked world, the only guarantee is uncertainty. The only way to meet it is by being curious."

DAVID EPSTEIN

WHEN THERE IS no definition, it is hard to determine direction. Where exactly do we start if we don't know what we are or are trying to be? As Generalists, we must begin with the existential yet pedestrian problem of invisibility before we can embrace a definition and direction. Understanding what's missing shapes our case for recognition and, more importantly, the types of support we need to meet the pressures of the time in which we live.

The specialization myth

In 2020, the author Malcolm Gladwell conducted a live audience interview with respected journalist and author David Epstein to discuss Epstein's recently published book, *Range: Why Generalists Triumph in a Specialized World*. The duo immediately hooked a curious audience with this question: Is excellence a product of relentless and focused effort or wide-ranging curiosity and experimentation?

This was not the first meeting of Gladwell and Epstein. Indeed, this conversation and the idea for David Epstein's book were both seeded in 2013 when Epstein and Gladwell first met as panelists at MIT's Sloan Sports Analytics Conference. Both avid runners, researchers, and sports fans, Epstein and Gladwell were well-positioned for a conversation on athletic excellence. Epstein had just published his first book, *The Sports Gene*, which examined the controversial question of genetics and training in athletic performance. Gladwell's 2008 bestseller, *Outliers: The Story of Success*, explored the making of "high achievers." And while part of their conversation focused on the expected debate between the "nature" of genetics and the "nurture" of practice, the 10,000-hour rule, popularized by Gladwell's book, was also discussed.

While Gladwell's definition was more nuanced in his book, many started to use a more popularized version of "10,000 hours" as an easy measure of excellence, a fail-safe way to claim expertise. If you did anything for the equivalent of 10,000 hours, you were "automatically" an expert. Yet Epstein wondered whether this was indeed true. Based on his work as a journalist for *Sports Illustrated* and other publications, he probed whether specialization guaranteed success. And if specialization did not result in success, what did? He explored the answer to this question in his second book, *Range: How Generalists Triumph in a Specialized World*. Published in 2019, the book was shortlisted for the *Financial Times* and McKinsey Business Book of the Year Award, named as one of five titles on Bill Gates' "Holiday Books 2020" list, and appeared on the bestseller lists of *The Wall Street Journal*, *The Washington Post*, and USA *Today*.

Like Gladwell's *Outliers*, Epstein's meticulously researched book included hundreds of data points and nearly as many stories of exceptional success, including the early specialization of children in chess, sports, and music. He starts his book with the origin stories of Tiger Woods and Roger Federer. Woods famously held a golf club in his hands before he was a year old and began playing golf at the age of three. Woods' early and singular focus on golf is a popular example of early specialization as essential to later success.

Federer's path to success tells a different story. Even though his mother was a tennis coach, Federer played a variety of sports as a child. He did not focus exclusively on tennis until he gave up soccer at the age of twelve. While both Federer and Woods have achieved the pinnacle of their respective sports, it is Woods' storied start, not Federer's "delay," that is known and adopted by parents and coaches worldwide.

In investigating this story and hundreds of others, Epstein argues that it is *not* specialization—the much-popularized 10,000 hours of focused practice—that is the frequent pathway to success. Instead, Epstein argues that success, as exemplified by Federer, is more often the result of a range of zigzag experiences in which one learns and adapts, becoming increasingly innovative in delivering improved solutions.

Epstein points to Generalists' deep curiosity and willingness to learn as reasons they excel in addressing the problems of a rapidly changing world. Complex issues that lack permanent solutions—such as climate change, viral epidemics, and international drug trafficking—cannot be solved by expertise alone. They demand the approach to solving problems that Generalists bring: curiosity, creativity, and adaptability to changing circumstances. Epstein forcefully concluded, "In a wicked world, relying upon experience from a single domain is not only limiting, it can be disastrous."[3]

In making the case for Generalists, Epstein succeeded in describing the Generalist experience so robustly that we, as Generalists, did not even need a definition to feel validated. At the same time it's essential to be "seen;" early acknowledgment's outsized importance does not replace what is still missing. Though visible, as Generalists we still lack a functional definition, adequate support, professional development opportunities, and a well-defined career path.

Indeed, everything in the work world—from job descriptions, to sourcing, vetting, and hiring candidates, to degrees, certifications, performance reviews, and promotions—is geared to Specialists and their areas of expertise. By contrast, Generalists operate in a world where titles do not align with abilities, certificates fail to capture knowledge, performance measures ignore our value, and, finally, practice is not an accepted area of expertise. While we have, as Generalists, lived with ambiguity for decades, the times we live in demand transparency on our core abilities: adaptability, curiosity, and creative solutions. As Epstein's book points out on every page, the time for Generalists is now.

Our interconnected world is characterized by constant change, infinite possibilities, and equally numerous distractions. Since the late 1800s, the work world has successfully responded to change through increased specialization characterized by focused expertise that has resulted in enhanced efficiency and growth. However, with the advent of knowledge work, globalization, technological innovations, AI, and many other factors, a rapidly changing, ambiguous, and complex world has quickly emerged. This new world necessitates a different response—one that is "ranging," adaptive, collaborative, and discerning. A Generalist response.

The heart of the dilemma

In O.C. Tanner's 2023 *Global Culture Report*, fifty percent of Americans identified as Generalists.[4] According to *Harvard Business Review*, ninety percent of 17,000 CEOs studied had general management experience.[5] The data points to a critical irony; while everywhere, Generalists are without a definition or direction and lack awareness and support. Yet our disappointments stem not from what we lack, but from the rollercoaster of success followed by letdown (Epstein's "zigzag"). Successes are easy to enjoy; it is the letdowns of role misalignment, poor cultural fit, boredom, creeping doubt, or unfavorable comparisons to Specialists that have significant consequences and negatively impact our confidence, earnings, and career trajectory.

The rollercoaster is not our only predicament; indeed, our wide-ranging dilemma as Generalists is neatly captured in the word itself: "Generalist" simultaneously means anything, possibly everything, and yet exactly nothing. The word purports a broad range of abilities and a can-do attitude as easily as it does a lack of focus and inability to make decisions.

Solid yet inexpert. Useful but undeveloped. Good. Never great. The ubiquitous "jack-of-all-trades, master of none." (A flawed interpretation, as we discover in Chapter 2.)

Why do you think you are a Generalist?

This lack of definition is further complicated by the fact that, as Generalists, we are each distinctive; shaped by our particular talents, interests, and life experiences. No two Generalists share the same path. We might take a deep dive into one career, learn everything about it, and emerge before diving into a new area of interest and career. Or we may have multiple roles within a single company. Perhaps, like Michelle, we pursue numerous and concurrent roles that align with our values and interests, or, like Charisse, we flourish in a start-up environment. As Generalists, we may thrive as leaders, entrepreneurs, CEOs, managers, or, like Nasir, as consultants. Indeed, our careers are as diverse as Generalists are unique.

"The voyage of the best ship is
a zigzag line of a hundred tacks."

RALPH WALDO EMERSON

Although needed, Generalists lack a definition, direction, and development to support individual growth and collective effectiveness. This is the heart of the Generalist dilemma. Ubiquitous and yet unseen. Needed but unnamed. In demand but underdeveloped. The reason for the dilemma? As stated earlier, *everything* about the work world—sourcing talent, job descriptions, roles, hiring, performance assessment, certifications, career ladders, professional development, promotion, and more—is geared to support and reward Specialists.

This focus on Specialists wouldn't matter much except for the increasing complexity of the times in which we live. For decades, Generalists have found ways forward without formal structures or support. Yet change is happening swiftly and unpredictably like never before, creating new and complicated challenges. The dynamic nature of this change requires both the adaptability and versatility of Generalists *and* the in-depth expertise of Specialists. Only together can Specialists and Generalists meet the demands of our time.

In addition to the demands of change, there is the question of effectiveness. What would it look like if we, as Generalists, received what Specialists have long had? What could be true if Generalists were seen, supported, and developed by managers, mentors, and colleagues? How could we, as Generalists, *best meet* the demands of our time? The complexity of the problems we face in our "wicked world" compels us to ask and answer these questions.

Three core attributes of Generalists

An awkward and painful moment for a Generalist is answering "What do you do?" We may respond with a rambling description of everything we have done, or the ambiguous "jack-of-all-trades," multi-hyphenate, "a doer," Renaissance thinker, utility player, unicorn, leader, hobbyist, dabbler, and more. Even those of us who have titles can be stymied when explaining our value and impact.

A Generalist is a catch-all term for many essential employees in every organization, describing individuals in various roles, including CEOs, chiefs of staff, COOs, senior leaders, and managers who work in strategy, project development, client engagement, partnership development, programs, marketing, talent acquisition, and operations. The lack of a functional definition means we, as Generalists, also lack a term that provides us with a shared context with room for more nuanced interpretation and personalization. It is not just being a Generalist that matters; what matters is how we are each uniquely a Generalist.

A functional definition provides us with language to increase our visibility and value, and find a meaningful way forward—a definition we need and can understand. As Generalists, we share three core attributes that, when understood individually and explored collectively, provide us with a framework and definition to understand who we are and how we communicate and grow as Generalists.

- **Generalists have "ranging" curiosity**. Generalists are first and foremost relentlessly curious. We love to learn about many different things, and each of us have a particular strain of curiosity. Our interests might range across and include people, ideas, questions, and various data and materials. The process of accessing our curiosity, acquiring and curating information—how we learn—is also individualized. We might learn through conversation, or prefer to read deeply, or observe intently about any and everything. Our broad curiosity differs from that of the Specialist who seeks a deep understanding of a single question or issue.

- **Generalists make creative connections between disparate data and phenomena**. Generalists will identify gaps, patterns, or systemic issues and propose solutions. We take a lateral (not linear) approach to making sense of existing and missing information, often generating new ideas and solutions to test. We may be the ones to step into the gap, manage across teams to address a larger challenge, or think more broadly about addressing a systemic need. We excel at practice and embrace testing ideas, piloting projects, and leveraging expertise to provide initial or next-level solutions so that all, including Specialists, can excel.

- **Generalists require variability and thrive in changing environments.** Work context is the ultimate determinant of a Generalist's success. Our ability to adapt and refocus our attention and curiosity demands environments that provide variability and freedom to learn, explore, practice, and test solutions. Environmental factors can include the company's industry, type, stage, and access to mentors, managers, and team members who understand and cultivate the company's values, thereby supporting its development. A dynamic environment is essential to a Generalist's success, development, and growth.

How can a definition help you with your particular "Generalist dilemma"?

These three main attributes can be distilled into a shorter functional definition:

Generalists are widely curious,
creatively connecting information
to ideate and test solutions,
address gaps, and solve problems.

While a functional definition helps, it alone does not solve the Generalist dilemma. As Generalists, we need the same access to structured support that is available to those who specialize. While there are some blog posts, articles, books, podcasts, and TED Talks that address the purpose and value of a Generalist, the quantity pales in comparison to the educational and professional offerings for specialized work. Professional development and growth are barriers for many Generalists. Currently, managers are tasked with unanswerable questions: How do I support a Generalist's development? What does their career look like? What skills do they need if not those of a Specialist? How do I give feedback or assess their performance if they are not an expert?

Though the focus is on Generalists, the impact is on everyone. Supporting Generalists is not just about Generalists: it matters to everyone in an organization, especially Specialists who depend on our adaptability to many roles and functions as crucial to shared success. As Generalists, we may be a CEO or chief of staff, lead strategy, run a division, collaborate across teams, develop staff, fill in gaps, spot opportunities, pilot programs, manage projects, carry company culture, coach, consult, or build a start-up or another function. Yet, regardless of the roles we play and the work we do, our understanding of and collaboration with Specialists is essential to every Generalist's success.

Generalists and Specialists: essential collaborators

The relationship between Generalists and Specialists has always existed. Specialists are defined by their expertise, rightfully valued and trusted for their deep knowledge and demonstrable skills. To become experts, Specialists follow a defined career path with competencies identified and assessed. For example, a plastic surgeon completes pre-med courses and then applies to, attends, and graduates from medical school. With a diploma in hand, they complete a required residency, followed by a fellowship at a hospital specializing in a subspecialty, perhaps reconstructive or cosmetic surgery. Even when performing surgeries regularly, they are required to participate in ongoing training and continuing education credits to ensure they remain current on evolving skills, technology, and knowledge. While the path to becoming a surgeon is not easy, the required knowledge, qualifications, assessments, expert mentors, and time demands are clearly defined. The progression is clear, and, perhaps most importantly, capabilities are tested and certified by other experts. Patients and hospital staff can trust and depend on the surgeon to perform their job effectively. The narrative of a Specialist aligns with their career: we see precisely how the novice becomes the expert, the student the Specialist.

Specialists accumulate knowledge through a focused curiosity, resulting in the expertise they bring to solving problems. A linear approach ensures they follow the steps, pass the tests, and maintain the protocols specific to their expertise. This linear approach is crucial in many situations, especially those where the outcome could have a disproportionate or hazardous impact, such as studies involving human subjects or laboratory experiments that utilize flammable materials. However, this linear approach used by industrialists—notably Henry Ford, who discovered efficiencies in specialization (shorter production times, fewer mistakes, safer processes)—has had an outsized impact on the work world we operate in today. The dominance of specialization as a means of both production and problem-solving has, in turn, shaped the education and work systems in which we all function. The result? Specialists receive extensive support through education, certification, promotion, and recognition, all structured to demonstrate a deeper and more precise understanding of their field.

While Generalists are the focus of this book, Specialists are essential to our success as our sources of information, collaborators in problem-solving, and sustainers of solutions. Like any symbiotic relationship, Generalists and Specialists are most effective when mutually supportive. Specialists benefit from the Generalist's adaptability and expertise as practitioners. Generalists attending to the vetting and testing of opportunities allow Specialists to focus and capitalize on their learning. In turn, Specialists provide Generalists with the fuel and knowledge that feeds our curiosity and sustains solutions. We see this dynamic at play everywhere when we pay attention. Generalists may, for example, lead the initial development of a new product or program, initially seeking input from sales on client feedback and processing insights from program leaders. They may conduct an external scan for best practices, competitors, and more, resulting in a development plan that relies on the expertise of the best as much as it does on creative ideas. The Generalist plays the roles of gap spotter, convener, and innovative problem solver. Similarly, a Specialist's function fills a role of expertise and execution, bridging information and operations. Together, they create the solutions and systems that can sustain, change, and scale in response to accelerating demands.

However, today the factors that accelerate change are inherently more complex and cannot be addressed with a linear, logical, step-by-step approach. Indeed, the thinking that led us to this point of complexity will not be the solution that enables us to respond and move forward.

How have Specialists played a part in your career?

The future is here. We are now in a time of rapid global change driven by AI and 'intelligent' computers, among other key factors. With the advent of ChatGPT and other AI engines, we are beginning to understand both the speed and scale of transformation we will experience over the next twenty years. The complexity and pace of change place unusual demands on employers, who must reskill and upskill their current employees while contemplating future demands and changes. According to the World Economic Forum, forty-four percent of employers believe that six in ten employees will need reskilling in 2027.[6] Reskilling is one need, adaptability to change, and the ability to flourish in the unknown will also be required. It is, as Epstein's book argues, the time for Generalists. Our curiosity, creative connections, and the ability to thrive in a fluid environment make us essential to navigating the ambiguous changes ahead.

What's next?

Recognizing our abilities as Generalists can be a game-changer for us individually, the people we work with, and the problems we best address together. We can each find satisfaction and success by better aligning our talents with opportunities and environments that foster our growth and encourage us to thrive.

Consider Charisse, who successfully reframed her failed expectations of permanent employment by embracing a consultant's perspective. Recognizing that she was energized when working in start-ups and subsequently lost steam when the organization stabilized, she decided to become a consultant, which for her meant working full-time for a start-up for six to twelve months, taking a month or two off to travel before starting a new job at another start-up. Then there is Nasir. His previous boss convinced him to return to his former firm, but this time in a senior role where he could once again leverage his strengths in scanning the landscape and assessing new opportunities while managing a team. He is still there today. Michelle, now living on land, has found, like Charisse, a niche as a consultant. Today, she focuses her curiosity on exploring and understanding other cultures and her clients' unique challenges, finding satisfaction in each discovery and developing tailored solutions that meet her clients' needs.

While each of the Generalists we met at the beginning of the book found a way to work that aligns with their value, it is in the collective where the promise of Generalists lives. As we will explore in Chapter 2, Generalists come from a long tradition of being needed during times of flux and change, but perhaps they are needed now more than ever.

KEY POINTS

- Generalists are largely invisible and unsupported everywhere.

- In many ways, the work world is geared to Specialists.

- Currently, there is no functional definition or shared understanding of a Generalist.

- Both Specialists and the demands of change need what Generalists bring: adaptability in ambiguous conditions.

- Core Generalist attributes include curiosity, creative connections, and context.

- Only together can Specialists and Generalists meet the demands of a changing world, economy, and workplace.

- Generalists need what Specialists have long had: frameworks, support, and growth aligned with their strengths (not just skills).

QUESTIONS FOR FURTHER REFLECTION

How have you succeeded as a Generalist?

_____

_____

_____

What is frustrating for you as a Generalist?

_____

_____

_____

Where might you grow as a Generalist?

_____

_____

_____

WORKBOOK

See sections 00 and 01
for additional exercises.

2

WHY WE NEED GENERALISTS

"To understand is
to perceive patterns."

ISAIAH BERLIN

FUTURISTS AND HISTORIANS, though attending to very different time frames, share a similar focus on patterns and trends and the importance of data and evidence: historians to make sense of the past and futurists to see beyond what is predictable. Trends are often dismissed as fleeting fads, but when viewed through the lenses of historians and futurists, they provide valuable insights, revealing a pattern that points to a deeper meaning. The idea of Generalists could be easily dismissed as a trend, a retread of grasping relevance. Yet history tells us otherwise. And while the future cannot yet be predicted, a deeper exploration of Generalists and current change gives us a pragmatic way forward. But first, a brief look back.

The hedgehog and the fox

The British political theorist, philosopher, and historian Isaiah Berlin borrowed Archilochus's evergreen parable of the hedgehog and the fox to capture the dynamic between Generalists and Specialists in his popular 1953 essay, "The Hedgehog and the Fox."[7] The cunning and creative fox, who "knows many things" (the Generalist), fails in every attack on the hedgehog (the Specialist), who "knows one big thing." The pragmatic maxim, "jack-of-all-trades," was wrongly credited to Benjamin Franklin (another Generalist). It was Robert

Greene, in his 1592 booklet *Greene's Groats-Worth of Wit*, who, with disdain, described Shakespeare in Latin as "Johannes Factotum or the 'johnny' [now jack] of all trades, master of one."[8] The quote referred to Shakespeare's many abilities (or vanities, as Greene saw it) as a prop maker, stage manager, and actor, and also his one main role, as playwright. The more recent, frequent, and less complimentary phrase, "master of none," became popular in the 1800s.

Jumping forward in time, we have the impact of scientific discoveries and the cultural creativity of the Renaissance (consider uber Generalist Leonardo da Vinci), and then two significant shifts that have contributed to the world we now live in: industrialization and specialization. Significant industrialization started with James Watt's improvement of the steam engine in England in the 1770s and, over the next 150 years, transformed how we produce what we need and use. While factories had existed before, their size and location depended on their power source, chiefly water from rivers; the steam engine could be used anywhere, resulting in the movement of people from land to factory-based work, impacting everyday living, social structure, and norms.

The steam engine and resulting technologies, especially the railroad, catalyzed the exponential growth of factories, industrialization, cities, and the population. In 1801, the population of London was just under a million people within a five-mile radius. A century later, 6.5 million people were living in a city 17.5 miles wide, filled with factories and multi-story buildings, and traversed by rail lines connecting to cities and ports.[9] Workers in early factories were responsible for many, if not all, parts of manufacturing—each accountable for starting and completing a product—just as they had been when they lived on the land. Attention to specialization, and its impact on manufacturing and production, did not occur until the early twentieth century with the advent of Henry Ford and his now infamous factory model.

In the 1910s, Henry Ford reverse-engineered and then applied the slaughterhouse process to car assembly. The change from a team working on one car to each worker specializing in a single part of production was revolutionary beyond the factory walls. His innovation reduced factory time required to build a car from twelve hours to ninety-three minutes, increased supply, made cars affordable, and accelerated both the modern industrial age and the rise of the middle class.[10] Many businesses soon followed Ford's model of specialization, expanding the economy, catalyzing new industries, and encouraging once-small companies to grow into large corporations.

While specialization dominated most of the twentieth century, there are more recent examples of Generalists. In 1956, General Electric launched a first-of-its-kind, three-year rotation program and training center for promising managers. The investment, at one time over $1 billion annually,[11] created a generation of Generalists who carried the company's core value of broad experience into leadership roles at GE and beyond. However, both the center and approach were short-lived and signaled the "end" of the Generalist for several decades.

In 1967, just ten years after GE created its program, Peter Drucker, heralded by *BusinessWeek* as the "man who invented management," published *The Effective Executive: The Definitive Guide to Getting the Right Things Done*. The book details five essential habits for executives and successfully argues for Specialists in an information economy, even at the cost of Generalists. Drucker was direct, stating, "The only meaningful definition of a 'generalist' is a specialist who can relate his small area to the universe of knowledge." He continued, "Maybe a few people know more than a few small areas. But that does not make them generalists; it makes them specialists in several areas. And one can be just as bigoted in three areas as in one. The man, however, who takes responsibility for his contribution will relate his narrow area to a genuine whole."[12] Drucker's influence and decades of teaching were popular with those who obtained MBAs, and the broad adoption of his principles further established specialization as the path to professional success.

In 2001, the metaphor of the fox and the hedgehog, introduced by Archilochus and deployed by Isaiah Berlin, resurfaced in Jim Collins' bestselling management book, *Good to Great*. But this time it had a different interpretation. In his book, Collins, an admirer of Drucker's, proposes the "Hedgehog Concept,"[13] arguing that the scattered thinking of the fox would result in less success when compared to the singular focus of the hedgehog. During times of change and challenge, he argues, organizations that focus on the single thing they are good at—their specialty—will survive and thrive. In the age-old debate of foxes versus hedgehogs, both Drucker's and Collins' encouragement of increased specialization left Generalists a largely ignored category, until recently. The information age is transforming rapidly in the era of intelligent computing (including artificial intelligence, virtual reality, and cloud technology), and has necessarily brought Generalists back into focus.

"Hope and curiosity about the future seemed better than guarantees. That's the way I was. The unknown was always so attractive to me... and still is."

HEDY LAMARR

Generalists make a comeback

Swiftly changing times have catalyzed a Generalist resurgence after decades where organizational skill and talent development favored Specialists. As we will discuss later, there are new career models, including the portfolio, squiggly, and fractional careers, that Generalists can embrace. There have also been a few attempts to identify and define types of Generalists. For example, in their book *The Neo-Generalist*, Kenneth Mikkelsen and Richard Martin argue that the Generalist is a serial Specialist. They include the examples of Hedy Lamarr, the actress and inventor who contributed to wireless communication, and the groundbreaking scientist Marie Curie, who won the Nobel Prize in both physics and chemistry. They describe Generalists as cycling through an "infinity loop" of curiosity, sparking a deep dive into one topic, which will then peak, and the loop will start anew with a different topic. The Neo-Generalist, they argue, is both a Generalist and a Specialist, "their generalist tendencies in service of deep specialisms."[14]

In technology, the need for Generalists has resulted in identifying several types—T, M, V, and I—along the Generalist-Specialist spectrum. T-shaped Generalists, sometimes referred to as Generalized Specialists, typically stay within their field and are highly valued in environments where specialized knowledge and collaboration are essential. For example, an engineer who has a deep understanding of the technology and also collaborates effectively with the sales team. The versatile V-shaped Generalist, increasingly popular in the user experience (UX) community, brings expertise in one or more areas and a more profound curiosity in adjacent areas. The M-shaped Generalist will often have an area of focus that ties together their multiple skills. For example, an entrepreneur who is focused on solving climate challenges may start a series of companies to address various climate-related problems. Finally, the I professional is the Specialist: their deep expertise in one area brings value to that role and field.[15]

Are you a "type" of Generalist? Why or why not?

If we were to revisit and reframe the parable of the fox and the hedgehog in today's world, we might start with the fact that both the ranging fox and the expert hedgehog are essential to meeting today's challenges. We might even push the metaphor further and ask less about who the fox and the hedgehog might represent, now that both are essential, and inquire instead about the changing environments in which they find themselves. What does the world need today that demands the best of both the fox and the hedgehog? How can we best anticipate and navigate the demands of a fast-changing and unpredictable environment?

History cannot predict the future, but it does help us understand the present and why Generalists are increasingly necessary and impossible to ignore. We have the lauded examples of well-known Generalists who thrived in their contributions during times of significant growth and change, including Shakespeare, Leonardo da Vinci, Henry Ford, Marie Curie, Hedy Lamarr, Steve Jobs, and many others. Each of these Generalists succeeded because their "ranging" curiosity and ability to make creative connections were needed to navigate exponential growth and change. This is also true today, when Specialists and society more broadly require what Generalists uniquely bring. Just as Specialists were essential to the exponential growth during the twentieth century, Generalists will be to how we successfully navigate the twenty-first century.

WHY WE NEED GENERALISTS   33

The time for Generalists is now

The past fifty years have witnessed dramatic transformations in the world of work. Individually owned businesses and mom-and-pop shops have given way to larger, hierarchical corporations with greater numbers of employees, resulting in a corresponding need for improved management. The advent of computers and the internet heralded the information age, a "Fourth Industrial Revolution" (the first three being steam, electricity, and information).[16] Computer intelligence—including artificial intelligence, machine learning, virtual reality, cloud computing, and more—is, with changes in biotechnology, rapidly transforming nearly every aspect of life, alongside challenges such as climate change, social divisions, and epidemics. We are living in a time of rapid and complex change with no easy answers; a time of what David Epstein rightly calls "wicked problems."

This is the world that Generalists did not necessarily build, but in which we can thrive.

In their 1985 book, *Leaders: The Strategies for Taking Charge*, the economists Warren Bennis and Burt Nanus developed a model to understand further what they considered the drivers of global change.[17] The VUCA model names four threats—volatility, uncertainty, complexity, and ambiguity—predicated on turbulence driven by an expected and significant increase in population, the consequential stress on natural resources, and major shifts in both power and climate. In 1990, the recent collapse of the Soviet Union prompted the US Army War College to adopt the VUCA model as a framework for responding to similarly unexpected future challenges. This was a significant decision, requiring a distinctly different skill set and organizational structure from leaders than those of centuries past (also captured in the acronym VUCA: Vision, Understanding, Clarity, and Agility).

A recent example is helpful. The VUCA theory anticipated the very kind of disorder the world experienced during the COVID-19 pandemic in 2020. Disrupting every facet of life, from travel to school, to work, to supply chains, the unseen virus prompted two generalized responses. There were those—individuals, companies, institutions, and organizations—who, once off track, struggled to move forward, while others found a way to adapt, pivot, and navigate the unpredictable. If we examine the impact on work alone, we see the emergence of a new and evolving normal—a way forward that is being piloted by those who can adapt, pivot, and perform. While not without challenges, remote and hybrid work are now the norm, and the once banal topic of global supply chain challenges has become an "everyone's problem." The challenges wrought by the pandemic are accompanied by others, contributing to a time of complex change.

To many, the future is depressing: a dismal world in increasing disarray with little opportunity for proactive engagement. Yet for many Generalists, current changes pique curiosity and the demand for new and different ideas. Although this may not seem like an opportunistic time, given the complexity and pace of change, it is precisely when Generalists are needed and more valued. Here is a brief overview of key challenges we, as Generalists, need to have some understanding of:

- **Technological acceleration**: The year 2024 may well be remembered as the year that marked the explosive growth and widespread use of AI, with the launch of GPT4 and Claude 3.5 Sonnet, while Perplexity AI achieved a valuation of over $1 billion (and an astonishing $15 billion just one year later). Artificial intelligence is and will continue to change our work in fundamental and profound ways; some of these changes we can anticipate, while others, for now, remain unknown. Other technological advances, including robotics, virtual reality, and biologically based technologies, will have similarly unpredictable impacts on every aspect of our lives. The need to discover how best to utilize these technologies in the service of human benefit is foundational to an improved future.

- **Multi-generational workforce**: In some workplaces, up to five generations are working together. This is a first, and the expectations, standards, and assumptions differ by generation, causing misunderstanding and friction for some, and talent and management issues for others. As many articles and opinion pieces suggest, preferences for professional development and learning opportunities vary across generations, as do preferences for recognition and rewards. While the differences in knowledge, expertise, and expectations presented by a multi-generational workforce can create a more complicated and challenging work environment, they can also be a profound source of untapped strengths and needed talent. Managers and others who engage across teams will need to increasingly identify and quickly implement strategies that support genuine connection and growth across generations, so that together we can meet the rapidly evolving demands.

- **Belonging**: While being responsive to multiple generations in the workforce is one way to promote belonging, the diversity of the workplace reflects changing demographics and an increased awareness, desire, and/or need, depending on the individual, to dismantle barriers to full engagement in the workplace. Paying attention to the myriad lived experiences of employees, regardless of age, background, or any other aspect of identity, is essential as we leverage our collective talent to meet the demands of our time. Additionally, the changes happening at work require different approaches and skills. Relational skills, which have historically been referred to as "soft skills" and are often regarded as optional, are essential to creating a thriving work environment and engaging employees.

- **Remote and hybrid work**: The pandemic normalized the concept of remote and hybrid work. There are benefits to both in-person and remote work, based mainly on the role and career stage. Remote and hybrid work benefits employees in several ways.

According to a 2023 Gallup study, eighty-five percent of fully remote workers report that an improved work-life balance is a significant benefit of remote work.[18] Yet being in the office allows for informal "water cooler" conversations that reinforce organizational culture and make it easier for managers to distribute work, assess productivity, and facilitate collaboration. A 2023 study by *The Wall Street Journal* revealed that ninety percent of CEOs "prioritize in-office employees for career-advancing projects, raises or promotions." The same report noted that full-time remote employees, especially women, were thirty-one percent less likely to receive a promotion and had fewer opportunities for development and mentoring.[19] That said, hybrid and remote work is here to stay. The opportunities and challenges will evolve as technology, types of roles, and external factors (including epidemics, climate change, and global connections) impact work.

- **Employee (dis)engagement and well-being**: Substantial data support the link between well-being and effectiveness at work, as well as the consequences of employee disengagement. While employee engagement can be challenging to promote, as the data suggests, it is essential to organizational success. Gallup recently added well-being—the overall quality of life, including physical health, emotional health, financial stability, social relationships, and sense of purpose—to its annual survey on employee engagement. Employees who are engaged *but not* thriving are sixty-one percent more likely to burn out often or always.[20] In a study of over 142 countries, Gallup data indicated that over half of the world's population feels at least somewhat lonely; a quarter of adults reported feeling very or fairly lonely.[21] Indeed, disruptions, like the recent pandemic, both increase loneliness and underscore the importance of well-being. Well-being, especially in a hybrid work world, is essential to an engaged workforce and an issue that companies must continue to address.

What changes in the workplace are you experiencing?

While globalization may make the world feel smaller, it has not always made it easier; accelerated information flows make change more difficult to metabolize. The new reality is that specialization is no longer enough to direct the rate and type of change characteristic of a VUCA world. Specialists need help. As Generalists, we are well-positioned to partner with Specialists to meet the demands of the time and explore the possibilities of utilizing new technologies, testing ideas, piloting solutions, or assisting others in adapting to change.

In addition to our curiosity, which helps us welcome and adapt during change, we also bring what are mistakenly called "soft skills." Soft skills are not "soft," but are essential; essential to communicating and collaborating successfully during the tense times characteristic of change. While the reskilling of employees and integration of new technologies (including AI) will meet and mitigate some of the demands of change, they alone are not enough. Essential skills are fundamental to the successful transformation of work. As we transition from the traditional "command and control" hierarchy to adaptive leadership, managers and leaders alike must cultivate a deeper understanding of relationships to ensure better decisions and more resilient cultures.

The definition and function of a Generalist is being both reintroduced and reinvented. It is no longer a jack-of-all-trades, utility player, or the default "go-to" when no one else knows what to do. A Generalist is a strategic role with many possible titles informed by key attributes and further defined by individual strengths and capabilities. Generalists are no longer relevant in a general way. Instead, each Generalist matters in a specific way to the colleagues we collaborate with, the challenges we take on together, and the change we seek to make.

Generalists are at a crossroads

We are at a time of decision: we can wait for companies, organizations, and talent leaders to identify and operationalize solutions, or we can, as Generalists, come up with our own. If we wait, we risk never getting what we need, or, when we do, it will be too little and too late.

Suppose we do drive the process of defining our value and finding a way forward. For reasons we are already too familiar with, we cannot be usefully categorized by what has benefited Specialists: skill level, titles, roles, and credentials. What if we took a different approach? One that asks: What would it look like if we explored the characteristics of Generalists and the conditions in which we thrive? What might we better understand as Generalists to help us be at our best, and what do we need to get there?

Epstein's book title, "Range: How Generalists Triumph in a Specialist World," immediately signals to readers that Generalists are anything but linear: we "range," seeking breadth rather than depth, in our lives, experiences, and work. We do not follow a predictable path or a ladder up, and often have careers in non-traditional models. As Generalists, we typically create an uncharted path, whereas Specialists necessarily travel paths paved precisely to ensure their expertise. Both roles are necessary, but the context is crucial. While Specialists can plan their careers, Generalists currently cannot.

The absence of career pathways cannot be underestimated. The lack of clarity, support, and value places Generalists at a higher risk of burnout, dead-end careers, and disengagement. In their 2023 study on global culture, O.C. Tanner described not only the rise of Generalists but also the needs they have. The report stated: "More than half (56%) of Generalists believe there is no clear career path for them, with 35% feeling excluded from promotions. This has an impact not only on their career trajectory but also on their total earnings. Nearly half (48%) say Specialists move up the career ladder faster." The report continued: "Some Generalists feel it's easier to see the goals and accomplishments of Specialists because their roles are more defined and specific."[22]

What needs do you have as a Generalist that have yet to be met?

What's next?

The question then becomes: If a "career path" fails Generalists, is there a model that can help? What would it look like for individuals to align their talents within the context of common Generalist characteristics? How would they thrive and succeed? While a path is necessarily linear, a framework allows one to self-direct and re-align. A Generalist framework that keeps curiosity, creative connections, and context as steadfast guidelines ensures that a Generalist's efforts are authentic, buildable, and highly individualized. A framework can promote individual growth, foster a nuanced understanding of key conditions, and support a shared sense of Generalist value. In Chapter 3, we will explore a framework that provides what Generalists have long needed: a way to confidently own their talents, develop their strengths, and craft a career narrative.

KEY POINTS

- Generalists have existed for millennia; their curiosity and creative connections catalyze, respond to, and shape change.

- Generalists are needed now to meet the complexity and challenges of global changes and demands.

- Generalists bring particular abilities to the skills needed now. These include:

  - People skills—understanding how to manage, motivate, and align people.

  - Problem-solving skills—testing ideas and finding solutions.

  - Possibility skills—discerning and deciding in a world of imperfect and/or changing circumstances.

- A definition and new model are needed that allow individual Generalists to name, claim, and develop their value proposition within the shared definition.

QUESTIONS FOR FURTHER REFLECTION

Are there examples of past Generalists who have inspired you?

What anticipated changes in the work world are of interest to you?

What gives you hope as a Generalist?

WORKBOOK

See section 02 for
additional exercises.

3

THE GENERALIST DEVELOPMENT FRAMEWORK

"Don't let anyone rob you of your imagination, your creativity, or your curiosity. It's your place in the world; it's your life."

MAE C. JEMISON

THE PAST 100 years have supported the ever-growing specialization in credentials, roles, and careers. By definition, Generalists
defy this taxonomy of expertise, leaving us without readily identi-
fiable titles, jobs, or career paths. To meet the demand for what
we can bring, we need an approach that is neither linear nor a ladder,
but still guides Generalists to career success. If we "reverse engineer"
what a Generalist is, we can bring meaningful dimension to the functional definition of "Generalist" by understanding what it means to
be *curious*, make *creative connections*, and, later, learn the importance
of the *context* in which we individually operate. Placing each of these
core attributes within a relational framework allows us to both
externalize "what" we are as Generalists and visually explore where
we might be in the development and effectiveness of our abilities.

A definition declares our existence while a framework brings
clarity and adaptability; both allow us to navigate our shared attributes and combine our strengths:

Generalists are widely curious, creatively
connecting information to ideate, test
solutions, address gaps, and solve problems.

Let's take a closer look at the first keyword here: "curious." Then, we will dive into what it means to be "creatively connecting" before looking at "context"—and how all three relate to form the Generalist framework.

Getting curious about curiosity

Animals are curious, and humans even more so. We are the only species to ask the question: "Why?" Curiosity is the essential currency of Generalists, just as knowledge is the currency of Specialists. In both his book *Range* and subsequent interviews, David Epstein identifies curiosity as the defining quality of a Generalist. Tim Harford refers to curiosity as the "golden rule" in his book *The Data Detective*.[23] Yale School of Law Professor Dan Kahan noted in his study of risk perception that curious individuals, regardless of their political identity, successfully facilitated conversations on the issue of political division.[24]

The power of curiosity is in challenging assumptions and seeking new possibilities. Yet in action, curiosity is often unruly, unbound, and even difficult. Curiosity powers our learning, and, with time, it demands not just application but also curation. Specialists ask questions to seek a deeper understanding of their expertise. As Generalists, our ranging curiosity helps us satisfy our need for variety, fuels our adaptability, and gives us what we need to address the problems we help solve.

"Be curious, not judgmental."

TED LASSO

While curiosity is the impetus to know more, the quality and reason behind that impetus can be differentiated based on motivation.

In the 1990s, George Loewenstein's research on curiosity yielded three distinct dimensions of curiosity.[25] The first kind of curiosity fills gaps, the second deepens knowledge, and the third alleviates boredom. In his book *Why? What Makes Us Curious*, astrophysicist and author Mario Livio points to two different kinds of curiosity, which the journalist Ian Leslie, in his book *Curious*, expanded to four: epistemic, perceptual, diverse, and, later, empathic curiosity. These four types of curiosity help us embrace the nuance of our curiosity. What, or who, are we interested in? And why?

- **Perceptual curiosity** is derived from surprise or missing information that prevents us from moving forward. Perceptual curiosity seeks answers that fill in gaps, allowing us to move forward with learning and understanding. In a podcast interview with Wharton Knowledge,[26] Livio describes perceptual curiosity as a little uncomfortable, "a bit like an itch that we need to scratch," with the answer giving relief. An example might be forgetting the name of a famous person, the discomfort that comes with trying to recall it, and the relief that comes with remembering.

- **Epistemic curiosity** is closely tied to knowledge acquisition, research, artistic creation, and the pursuit of a deeper understanding. Characterized as inquisitive, this type of curiosity is satisfied by knowing more. Specialists often exhibit this kind of curiosity as they seek to acquire expertise. Generalists flex this type of curiosity when seeking a deeper understanding of a topic.

- **Empathetic curiosity** is about how others think and feel and encourages our understanding of and connection with others. Empathetic curiosity pushes us to 'put ourselves in their shoes,' and, according to Leslie, is a curiosity that can and should be cultivated in ourselves and others. Empathetic curiosity helps explain Generalists who are particularly effective people managers.

- **Diverse curiosity** is fleeting and novel in nature. It is familiar to many as the motivation behind scrolling through a phone, clicking on a headline, or browsing an antique store. It is also the curiosity behind thrill-seeking, such as parachuting from a plane. This type of curiosity may keep boredom at bay, but it does not engage us in deeper exploration.

Which definitions of curiosity resonate for you?

As Generalists, understanding where our curiosity comes from helps us better direct our questions and learning. It also deepens our awareness of why we might, for example, be interested in understanding people (empathic curiosity), which differs from the kind of curiosity that drives a love of learning (epistemic curiosity). In Chapter 4, we will delve deeper into how our strengths influence our learning process and the types of curiosity we might use and need.

"A scientist in his laboratory is not a mere technician: he is also a child confronting natural phenomena that impress him as though they were fairy tales."

MARIE CURIE

Making creative connections

In solving math equations and conducting science experiments, we employ linear thinking: a step-by-step analysis that leads to a logical conclusion. Linear thinking is rational, consistent, and fail-safe, with step-by-step formulas to follow. Effective in solving cause-and-effect problems, linear thinking is less effective in addressing complex and systemic issues. Complex problems require creative and indirect reasoning to produce solutions that only seem obvious in retrospect. What we often refer to as "out-of-the-box thinking."

The concept of "out-of-the-box thinking" was first introduced by the Maltese physician and author Edward de Bono in 1967.[27] De Bono tested "what if" scenarios and identified "intermediate possibilities" reached through initial experimentation, resulting in solutions for further testing. A pattern will emerge from this iterative process, de Bono explains in *Lateral Thinking*, the book with the title of the term he invented. He wrote, "With alternate thinking, the blocks are scattered around. They may be connected loosely or not at all. But the pattern that will eventually emerge will be as useful as the vertical structure."

Dan Kahneman's bestseller, *Thinking, Fast and Slow*, popularized the idea of fast (System 1) and slow (System 2) thinking.[28] System 1 thinking can be described as the brain's automatic, unconscious, and reflexive response; the "unthinking" behind actions such as brushing one's teeth, avoiding a pothole, and scanning social media. System 2 thinking is "slow" and deliberate and is used when the brain seeks to solve more complicated challenges; the focus is on selecting an allergy-free lunch, finding a known face in a large crowd, or navigating the shortest path through a crowded sidewalk.

Creative Connections
(Lateral Thinking)

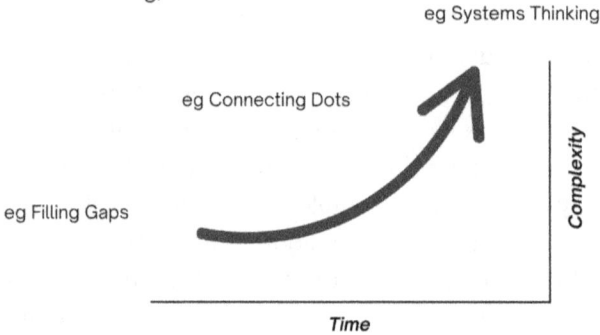

eg Systems Thinking

eg Connecting Dots

eg Filling Gaps

Complexity

Time

©BigSeaStrategies

These two models of thinking—lateral and fast/slow—help explain how Generalists make "creative connections." Generalists approach sense-making and problem-solving by seeing "the whole" and quickly identifying what might be missing, consistent, or aligned. This explains Generalists' ability to swiftly identify gaps, information vacuums, patterns, and systemic problems. While important in addressing complex issues, lateral thinking does not address every complicated problem. For example, a surgeon, a Specialist by any definition, brings linear thinking to the difficult work of operating, following one specific step after another to ensure a safe procedure and a healthier patient.

When it comes to making creative connections, three general categories differ in terms of timeline, proximity, and complexity. Identifying and filling gaps or information vacuums is the most straightforward approach. Connecting dots (one way of detecting patterns) is more complex, while systems thinking and solutions (bigger picture patterns) are the most complicated and have a longer timeline.

What kinds of problems do you seek to solve, and what kinds of "creative connections" do you make?

- **Identifying (and filling) gaps**: Some Generalists, when recognizing a problem, will quickly step in to mitigate or manage so others can continue their work and ultimately complete the task, achieve the objective, or meet the deadline. In addition to meeting the need, we might improve a process, address an underlying cause while, for example, doing work that there is no staff for (i.e., creating an HR manual or hiring staff), serving in an interim role (i.e., interim marketing director when a search for a replacement is in process), or helping a team meet an urgent deadline. Gaps can be informational, operational, or organizational, and between people, teams, ideas, and execution. Again, identifying and filling gaps happens quickly and for brief periods.

- **Connecting the dots**: "Connecting the dots" is the ability to discern patterns between seemingly unconnected or disparate phenomena. This is neither linear nor logical, but the ability to determine a pattern or "see" a solution that emerges from disparate information. Connecting the dots can occur within or across teams, addressing recent, interim, or more profound problems. This may involve borrowing solutions from other industries, reassigning teams based on projects, and devising new processes to address client needs.

- **Systems thinking**: As outlined in Peter Senge's book *The Fifth Discipline*,[29] systems are by definition interconnected. Systems thinking seeks to understand the whole picture—the entire system—while identifying the underlying problems. Those who think in terms of systems will often "zoom out" and ask "bigger picture" questions about the context and connected questions, such as "What other factors contribute to the problem?" While initially focused on addressing one problem, systems thinkers may find another that takes priority and needs a different solution; one that may even address more than one problem. The time required for systems thinking and solutions typically occurs over a long period, spanning years to decades, depending on complexity and other factors.

While these approaches differ in their immediacy, complexity, and time demands, they all share a creative, lateral, or "out-of-the-box" approach to solving problems. Whether we take a systems approach, spot patterns, or see gaps, as Generalists, we detect what is missing, not working, or needs improvement, and apply our knowledge and curiosity to find and improve solutions. Tackling complex problems by working within and across teams to shared success is when we are at our best.

Context: Conditions for success

Unlike curiosity and creative connections, we cannot control our work environment; only discern and decide what works best for us. A work environment comprises many factors: physical nature and type of work (office layout, remote and hybrid work), managers, colleagues, size and stage of an organization, leadership, and what we cannot see but feel: purpose, culture, and values. When lacking the support Specialists receive, Generalists are more dependent on work environments to meet our needs, and allow for our core capabilities to be expressed and utilized.

Like most employees, we often focus on a specific industry, field, size, or stage of an organization. Start-ups and multinational corporations offer different options in terms of size, scale, opportunities, and roles. Start-ups frequently hire Generalists, as they perform multiple roles and fill in the gaps in a quickly growing company. Many entrepreneurs themselves are Generalists. We also thrive in corporations, including in senior leadership roles, such as chiefs of staff, project managers, and key players on teams. Those of us in corporations often find interesting "inside" opportunities due to growth, leadership changes, staffing adjustments, and shifts in objectives and goals. Ultimately, many of us opt to work as independent consultants, coaches, or in fractional roles, selecting career models that align with our interests and work preferences.

Dr. Diane Hamilton, creator of the Curiosity Code Index,[30] also coined the apocryphal acronym FATE (fear, assumption, technology, environment) to identify the conditions in which curiosity fails to flourish:

- **Fear** of looking incompetent to others because there isn't room for error (and therefore no room for experimentation).

- **Assuming** others will not be interested in our curiosity discourages exploration.

- **Technology** is a barrier to curiosity rather than an aid.

- The **Environment** actively discourages, rather than encourages, exploration.

A highly structured environment, in which everyone is clear about their role and responsibilities, is necessary for functions in which accuracy and consistency are essential. For example, a scientist who is testing a hypothesis must adhere to specific protocols to ensure the validity and usability of their results by others. As Generalists, we excel in working across an organization and are exposed to and often impacted by more of a company's environment than others might be. We can borrow Diane Hamilton's acronym, "FATE," to determine the ideal environment for a Generalist to flex their curiosity and creative connections: freedom, ask (curiosity), test, and employ.

- **Freedom (not fear)**: Freedom allows us to seek variety, and align our abilities and strengths with possibility and impact. Indeed, freedom is arguably the most important factor we should consider as Generalists when assessing a possible work environment. While freedom is not a blanket license to do anything or everything, it can be the difference in maximizing our strengths, developing trust, and piloting possibilities. It is up to each Generalist to determine their preferred type of freedom.

- **Ask (not assume)**: As Generalists, we ask questions to satisfy curiosity and build knowledge while strengthening our ability to listen and discern. Having the freedom to ask, explore, and inquire can be fulfilled through a variety of roles, projects, and related opportunities that allow for learning and innovation. Large organizations can support Generalists by providing opportunities to work in various departments and teams across the organization.

- **Test (not technology)**: The value we bring as Generalists lies in our practice of helping to find and test solutions to emerging and persistent challenges. Generalists can leverage AI, machine learning, and other technologies to support the discovery of out-of-the-box solutions that enhance and complement the value of Specialist expertise.

- **Exploration (not environment)**: Environments that support learning, with effective feedback and permission to test and pilot new ideas, are a good fit for many Generalists. Opportunities to collaborate, whether in start-ups, cross-department projects, pilot efforts, or other initiatives, are typically a good fit.

Chapter 6 delves into context in depth, exploring the types of feedback and support Generalists need to develop their careers, effectiveness, and growth.

How do the key attributes of curiosity, creative connections, and context change your perspective of your abilities and career?

The Generalist Development Framework

Even with these deeper definitions of our key abilities, we desire, like our Specialist colleagues, a clear way forward. Yet, too often the path we follow is "the wrong one." We muddle through a job, skills misaligned, until disappointment creeps in and discouragement follows. Some of us, like entrepreneurs, find a way forward regardless. However, to meet present and future challenges, we can't leave Generalists on the sidelines or to their own devices. We need a new way for Generalists to find their path, meaning, and success.

By ditching the confines of a linear path in favor of a framework, we achieve two key shifts in thinking that enable Generalist success. A framework provides definitions and development so we can become competent as Generalists, individually discerning a dynamic path of both learning and success. A framework helps us deepen our understanding of who we are and what we bring, and promotes experimentation and learning. By having a framework that guides, not directs, we learn how to better our superpowers and guard against the pitfalls that crash so many Generalist careers: defaulting to Specialist career "ladders," failing to manage many interests, habitually operating via "fast" thinking, and choosing the wrong working environment.

While there is no single path for all Generalists, there is one framework that works for every Generalist.

Introducing: The Generalist Development Framework

Where Specialists have a pathway to expertise, a framework provides Generalists with the means to understand and develop how curiosity, creative connections, and context constitute who we are and can be as Generalists.

Generalist Development Framework

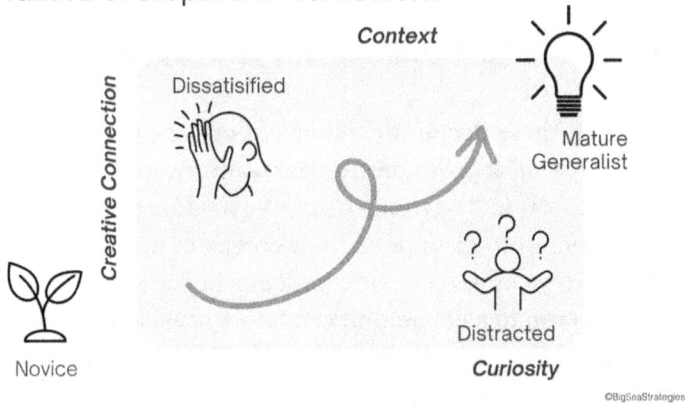

©BigSeaStrategies

To ensure simplicity and direction, the two attributes we can self-direct are mapped to the X and Y axes: "Curiosity" is the X-axis, and "Creative Connections" is the Y-axis. Our growth as Generalists, never linear, squiggles as we grow and develop through four unbounded categories: Novice (where we all start), Distracted (when curiosity is excessive), Dissatisfied (when a solutions-only focus and even impostor syndrome are at play), and Mature Generalist (our best, most informed version of our Generalist superpowers). These categories do not define or label us as much as they help guide our growth.

The third characteristic for Generalists, "Context," speaks to the conditions of an enabling environment for Generalists, specifically the kinds of workplaces in which a Generalist thrives. Context is discerned, not directed, and necessarily serves as the larger frame in which we operate. The more aligned we are with all attributes, both those we can self-direct and those we can discern, the better positioned we are to succeed as Generalists.

> "The more you learn,
> the more you have a framework
> that the knowledge fits into."
>
> **BILL GATES**

Unlike a signed path or ladder, this framework establishes the boundaries of what a Generalist needs to understand and self-manage—capabilities and context—to be effective. Thinking about each definition as a borderless garden helps us self-assess our effectiveness and identify areas to invest and improve.

The objective for all Generalists is to be a Mature Generalist. While different in detail for each of us, we become Mature Generalists when we understand that our growth is never static nor linear; that each attribute has inherent value, and different circumstances may require us to lean into one more than the other. We are Mature Generalists when we seek awareness, not balance, and commit to the idea of expert practice and active reflection.

Below is an overview of the four Generalist categories. Further guidance on careers and development for all categories will be covered in Chapters 6 and 7.

The Novice
The Novice is either someone new in their work journey or newly arrived at their Generalist path of discovery. While everyone new

to the work world is a Novice, a Novice Generalist is new to the realization that they are indeed a Generalist and not a (misplaced) Specialist. The Novice "garden" is experimental and overgrown, with no clear organization in terms of layout or plant types. While intriguing, a Novice Generalist can get stuck and confused if they do not develop self-awareness and intentionally own their curiosity, hone their ability to make connections, or pay attention to the context in which they thrive.

A Novice Generalist:

- Constantly asks questions
- Tends to "popcorn" ideas that are interesting but often disconnected from the problem at hand
- Leaps from one question to the next without pause
- Verbalizes their thought processes as a means of contribution
- Fails to ask next-level, more profound questions, or asks too many questions
- Does not listen with intention or discernment, missing nuance and key details
- Is initially enthusiastic but can quickly lose interest
- Can be uninterested in improving upon solutions
- Has no understanding of their ideal work environment
- Confuses shared attributes with individual talents and strengths
- Does not always know when and why they are successful
- Does not know how to ask for or use relevant feedback
- Needs and benefits from having a mentor who understands their talents
- Tries to succeed and then fails at the Specialist role more than once

Like any beginner, a Novice Generalist can be intentional about every aspect of their learning. They might focus on specific qualities and skills, prioritizing those they use more regularly, and seek mentors and others who can lead by example and provide feedback relevant to Generalists. Courses or classes can be a good option for skills related to their role. Establishing a habit of active daily or weekly reflection is encouraged. Tracking what was tried, the results, and the impact helps greatly. When well supported, the Novice can more quickly align their strengths and map a path forward to becoming their unique version of a Mature Generalist.

The Distracted

More mature in their understanding of being a Generalist than the Novice, the Distracted Generalist fully embraces their curiosity and is invigorated by moving from one new subject to the next. They ask great questions, have deep knowledge about many topics, and some may curate their knowledge; others may not. The Distracted Generalist values a high level of freedom to explore and, when bored, quickly moves on to the next interest. If the Distracted were a garden, it would be lush yet wildly overgrown, with only the gardener able to distinguish which plant was which, where each one was located, and what might be edible or not. There is a reputational risk associated with being a Distracted Generalist for being "only" curious, and they must guard against their questions as a distraction or learning for learning's sake. The Distracted Generalist can get trapped in pursuing endless and useless information or issues they cannot impact. If they pursue learning only at the cost of application, they may struggle to become effective Generalists.

A Distracted Generalist:

- Loves learning and has broad-based knowledge
- Loves to research, prepare, and start, but never quite "finish" a project

- Serves as a generative partner for ideas and possible solutions

- Is relentlessly curious about ideas, people, or processes

- Goes deep, asking follow-on and sequential questions

- Listens to learn

- Quickly moves from one idea to the next, asking many questions and absorbing the answers

- Deep dives into a subject area or surface, then immediately dives into another

- Spends too much time learning

- Has lots of disparate information about many subjects

- May or may not have a way to curate and organize learning

- Makes a great trivia partner

- Benefits when working with application-oriented partners

The Distracted Generalist benefits from partners and colleagues who need, and can effectively direct, their curiosity. Distracted Generalists should make an intentional effort to understand the types of problems they are interested in, how they approach problems, and the nuances of piloting, testing, and implementing solutions. Their love of learning and contributions to innovation and ideation benefit from having a system to curate their knowledge, including hobbies and topics for personal enjoyment.

The Dissatisfied

While the Distracted is defined by their relentless curiosity and relative lack of interest in solutions, the Dissatisfied is a Generalist who leans into their ability to decide on solutions by quickly identifying gaps, connecting the dots, or seeing the big picture. If the Dissatisfied were a garden, it would appear to be designed by a landscaper, seemingly perfect. Yet upon further investigation, it would become evident that someone created the garden themselves. The Dissat-isfied Generalist says yes to every problem ("I can do that!") and proceeds quickly with solutions, often with an immediate strat-egy, ideas, and their own opinions about what needs to change or be done. They may either ignore their curiosity or use it uninten-tionally, which hinders their ability to lead effectively as a Mature Generalist. They often side-step next-level questions or tangentially related issues in favor of swift action, eager to implement a solution and bypass others, including colleagues and managers.

The Dissatisfied Generalist can appear to do everything, yet often suffers from burnout when they fail to leverage the expertise of others and carry on doing the work alone. The Dissatisfied can appear as a frustrated Specialist by trying to fit in and accept performance measures that do not align with their strengths. They may experi-ence initial success but rarely have enough freedom to test ideas or pilot solutions, nor are they self-aware enough to learn from them.

A Dissatisfied Generalist:

- Identifies and seeks to solve problems quickly and independently

- Understands what kind of problems they seek out

- Sees the gap and moves quickly into action, often alone, as it is the "fastest way"

- Is interested in risk but often pursues it independently

- Pilots and implements solutions, but is bored with maintenance

- Says yes and rarely no, leading to burnout

- Suffers from impostor syndrome (often thinking they are a Special-ist who hasn't quite found their niche)

- Executes well, but not favorably when compared to Specialists

- Sees relentless curiosity as distracting, disruptive, and unpro-fessional

- Can be a good partner for the relentlessly curious

As the type of Generalist that most suffers from feeling like an impostor, the Dissatisfied Generalist benefits from managers who take a coaching approach to both model and develop their curiosity and focus on solutions. Dissatisfied Generalists can be good partners to other Generalists who are extremely curious, and make compelling people managers once they are confident in their own abilities and strengths.

The Mature Generalist

An effective Generalist is neither a role nor a destination, but an active balance between attention and implementation. Mature Generalists are self-aware and in command of their curiosity, insights, and ability to bridge information and action. They confidently ask the right kinds of questions, listen attentively, and know how to strike a balance between learning and decision-making to ensure action even with insufficient information. Like any good gardener, they understand the dimensions of their plot and are constantly practicing, testing, and adapting with new plants, but always with the bigger vision and design clear in their mind.

Mature Generalists understand the diversity individuals bring and how to align their strengths with the organization's goals and intended impact. They are often, though not always, leaders of an organization or a team. While their self-knowledge and management are essential, the most significant skill of a Mature Generalist is their discernment around decisions, especially when lacking complete information. Mature Generalists value learning from both success and failure, are quick to pivot or adapt, and allow others to do the same.

Mature Generalists know how their strengths amplify Generalist attributes and recognize (and even create) the kinds of environments in which they meaningfully thrive. Mature Generalists are aware of how they learn and curate their knowledge, and leverage their curiosity and ability to think strategically. As a result, they are intentional about their learning, communication, and decision-making.

A Mature Generalist:

- Is committed to best practices for practitioners, including a learning mindset

- Skillfully adapts

- Knows where and how they function best

- Has a nuanced understanding and keen control of their curiosity

- Curates and applies knowledge judiciously

- Identifies and seeks to solve problems quickly and inclusively

- Will play with ideas and test solutions

- Takes considered risks and understands failure as a learning

- Moves from role to role with intention

- Understands the capacity of self and others

- Has strong "people" skills

- Often leads or manages teams, projects, or organizations

- Possesses strong decision-making skills, even with missing information

- Knows what they need to succeed

- Depends on and supports Specialists

- Quickly spots talent and mentors Generalists

Our learning as practitioners is necessarily dynamic and without rigid boundaries. We adapt, change, and grow daily, weekly, and yearly just as gardens do. Feedback and reflection highlight where we are excelling, where we need to focus, and how best to chart our path and development. The true north, of course, is for each of us to become our version of a Mature Generalist. However, as you will discover in the following chapters, the pathway is neither straight nor narrow.

What's next?

The Generalist Development Framework maps Generalist core attributes, enabling us to develop our value proposition, identify areas for development, and align career objectives. In understanding the core attributes, we quickly begin to recognize where we excel and where we need to develop further. While we are all curious, it is more powerful to understand our type of curiosity. Do we want more information, connection, or is it a cognitive itch that needs to be scratched? Do we identify gaps, connect the dots, or sense patterns when scanning for opportunities and challenges? And what examples support what we sense or see? And, finally, what about context? How do we understand our ideal work environment today and, as we deepen our self-awareness and abilities, tomorrow?

In the next chapter, we will explore why strengths—not skills—are the tools of Generalists. Knowing how our strengths align with and are expressed as Generalist attributes allows us to understand what we uniquely bring, incorporate feedback, and identify growth opportunities.

KEY POINTS

- A framework works for Generalists as a pathway works for Specialists, providing a way to understand mastery of key attributes.

- The core attributes that support Generalist adaptability and value are:

  - Curiosity—allows for continuous learning, cross-pollination, and curation.

  - Creative connections enable disparate connections and "out-of-the-box" thinking and solutions, connecting dots and people across silos and departments, facilitating problem-solving—qualities of environments in which Generalists thrive.

  - Context—while we cannot control context, we can be mindful of it, as context can make or break a Generalist's success.

- The Generalist Development Framework enables Generalists to map their stage of development better. Like a garden, each is different, but boundaries are porous. The four categories are:

  - Novice—New in their work journey or newly arrived on the Generalist path.

  - Distracted—Curiosity is high, and they are less intentional about solving problems.

  - Dissatisfied—Seeking a solution and speed, withholding curiosity as a result.

  - Mature—Intentional in cultivating curiosity, making and testing connections within environments in which they can thrive and help others do the same.

QUESTIONS FOR FURTHER REFLECTION

What information, insights, or feedback helps determine your current place in the Generalist Development Framework?

_____

_____

_____

How will you approach the following chapters based on your framework insights?

_____

_____

_____

Which of your attributes do you think are underdeveloped or overused?

_____

_____

_____

WORKBOOK

See section 03 for
additional exercises.

4

THE POWER OF
PRACTITIONERS

"We learn who we are
in practice, not in theory."

DAVID EPSTEIN

HAVING A MAP, whether in hand or as an app on your phone, is an invitation to exploration and daydreams. We zoom in on desired locations, trace our finger along backroads to possible destinations, and estimate how far and how long travel might take to get from here to there. And yet, as informative and even inspiring as a map is, it falls short of capturing what our journey may be like. We can each use the same map, follow the exact directions, and yet have entirely different experiences. Our individual preferences, likes, dislikes, abilities, and strengths make each journey unique. This is as true of visiting a new place as it is in understanding who we are as Generalists and the power of being experts in practice.

Experts in practice

What do you do for work? For some, it's an easy answer: a chef, caretaker, doctor, data analyst, park ranger, or CEO. For others, especially Generalists, it is a dreaded question. Even with a title, we often struggle to provide an answer to the simple question: "What do you do?" When we try to explain, our efforts confuse rather than clarify, negatively impacting job searches, promotions, and networking opportunities. And yet our endeavor to seemingly self-sabotage does not stop there. When we try to substitute a detailed explanation with a variation of "I do everything and anything," we cause more confusion than if we had said nothing at all. While an enthusiastic response to figuring out any challenge of interest is a hallmark of a Generalist, enthusiasm alone fails to communicate the value we bring.

Lacking a universally known definition for "Generalist," we are stuck between two unhelpful responses: a lengthy, meandering description or the brief and meaningless answer of "a jack-of-all-trades." Yet our inability to answer this so-called simple question has real-world consequences, damaging our confidence and costing us connections and opportunities. The truth is, we lack an adequate answer to this question because it speaks to a Specialist's experience and expertise. As Generalists, we need a different question, one that we can answer adequately and confidently:

How do I make a difference? Our work as Generalists does not always fit into the measures of Specialist success: clear roles and responsibilities delivering measurable KPIs, outputs, outcomes, and revenue. The "difference we make" reframe allows Generalists to map how we contributed, collaborated, catalyzed, coordinated, managed, and supported the process, team, and client to impact. In a world of individual goals, outcomes, and promotions, our value often goes unrecognized because our day-to-day work is usually unplanned and unseen, existing between objectives and dependent on the collaboration of others. As Specialists deliver their measurable expertise, our expertise as Generalists lies in practice itself.

What does it mean to be an expert in practice? Specialists become experts through intentional learning and repetition of skills, as they practice their area of specialty. Doctors, teachers, and pastry chefs apply their specialist expertise: the plastic surgeon successfully reconstructs a nose, the teacher provides pedagogically aligned instruction, and the pastry chef consistently produces a perfect and flaky crust. Generalists take a similar approach to *practice* by intentionally improving their ability to try, adapt, and pivot to meet the demands of their role and change more broadly.

As Generalists, we strive to be experts in tackling challenges with innovative approaches and curated ideas: how to explore, collect, curate, pilot, initiate, revise, refine, experiment, modify, and adapt to address gaps, solve problems, and overcome challenges. Everything we do as Generalists has something new—a new approach, a new condition, a new idea, a new team—whether we are innovating, testing, or implementing. And the work we do is both dependent on and provides platforms for Specialists to further their expertise. By embracing practice as our shared expertise, we have the cornerstone of our value and clarity on our lifelong development as wide-ranging learners, attentive curators, effective collaborators, and discerning problem solvers.

Practice is intentional, not incidental, and requires learning through finessing what works and improving upon what doesn't. How we practice becomes our calling card and reputation. To be effective as a practitioner we must have at least a degree of self-awareness and self-management, which is why we first start with understanding our strengths.

A strengths-based approach

Whether a Specialist, Generalist, or something in between, we each bring a unique mix of inherent strengths and acquired skills to our work. At times confused with strengths, skills are learned: a chef's knife skills, an accountant's facility with spreadsheets, and a lawyer's ability to argue case law are all learned skills. A Specialist's skill level defines their role. Everyone expects a chef to be an expert in filleting a fish and a lawyer to know the nuances of law. Strengths (or talents) differ from skills; they are intrinsic and uniquely expressed. For example, while all chefs have knife skills, one chef may be particularly inventive in creating a daily special, and another may be renowned for their consistency in preparation and presentation. A lawyer with an analytical bent may structure a rational argument, whereas another may excel at appealing to a jury's emotions. Our strengths, whether we are Specialists or Generalists, point the way to discerning what makes us unique.

And yet, improving our performance at work has typically focused on what we don't do well. For years, the idea of being "well-rounded" defined effective performance and types of professional development. Then in 1999, Don Clifton, creator of Gallup's Clifton-Strengths,[31] prompted a game-changing question about improving human performance. What if, he asked, instead of spending so much time solving what is wrong about a person—their weaknesses—the focus was on what is *right* about a person? What would happen if people intentionally improved in the ways they were already naturally inclined? Don Clifton's proposition—that excellence is more easily achieved when we work from our strengths—has informed many strengths-based assessments, including the one he created, CliftonStrengths, which is used by tens of millions of people worldwide.

The idea of starting with "what is right" about us is transformative. An asset-based approach frees us to operate from our natural strengths while better managing, rather than wasting time investing in our "weaknesses." Utilizing our strengths fundamentally increases our self-awareness and ability to find success: excellence, not perfection, is the goal. The data on the effectiveness of using one's strengths supports Clifton's original premise, as do endorsements from leaders, including Adam Grant and others who advocate for a strengths-based approach to development.[32]

According to Gallup, employees who learn about their strengths are nearly eight percent more productive. When a team utilizes its talents daily, it becomes twelve-and-a-half percent more productive.[33] Gallup's research also discerns measurable improvements in key indicators, including engagement, satisfaction, and profitability. And while a strength-based approach benefits individuals, it also provides a shared language and framework helpful to team communication, feedback, development, and performance.

Knowing our strengths is not just helpful, but essential for Generalists. Skills serve as the default taxonomy for Specialists, mapping to roles and titles, with sequencing indicating expertise. In the job market, Generalists are unfavorably compared with Specialists, as expertise beats expediency when it comes to skills and related competencies (and the search engines that seek the same). And when we try to fit into a Specialist taxonomy, it obscures both the need and value of what we, as Generalists, bring.

What can we do?

Strengths don't define who we are; instead, it's our experience, industry, and the variabilities in geography, identity, and life experience that shape us. However, a strengths-based approach helps Generalists define our value proposition, much like how skills define Specialist value. In other words, strengths are to Generalists what abilities are to Specialists. Strengths enable us to individualize the Generalist framework of curiosity, creative connections, and context while finessing who we are as practitioners. Strengths are effective when intentionally flexed and as a tool for pursuing further growth and development. It is our strengths that answer the question "Where do we excel?" with a response that clarifies rather than confuses.

Assess and ask

So, where to start? It's hard to identify one's strengths, which is why we should use an assessment tool or survey our colleagues. Both of these actions give us insights we cannot easily discern ourselves.

Any assessment should be approached with cautious optimism. Assessments are indicators, and provide just one type of feedback to further self-awareness. While paid strengths-based assessments—such as CliftonStrengths, Hogan Assessments, and the VIA (Values in Action) Survey of Character Strengths—differ in some ways, they share a focus on what is right about you, a ranked order and detailed descriptions of talents, and access to learning materials. A paid (or free) assessment is valuable in that it mitigates collegial bias and provides a list of top strengths to interrogate and integrate. And while helpful, these assessments do not take into account individual lived experiences, background, education, and other factors that shape who we are. The final determination of strengths in play—and how we choose to adopt or use them—is entirely up to us.

Asking colleagues, clients, classmates, direct reports, friends, and managers—past and present—is another helpful way to ascertain one's strengths. Their observations of our impact are more objective than ours can be, allowing for a consensus to form on both key and lesser strengths. When 5-10 (or more) colleagues are asked, clear themes and specific words emerge—evidence of an agreed-upon strength. Assessments and feedback coalesce into an externalized understanding of who we are, allowing us to enhance our self-awareness, apply our strengths, find flow, and improve performance.

Map strengths to key attributes and conditions

Our strengths help explain our unique curiosity, creative connections, and context. This more nuanced and individualized understanding of our strengths informs our narrative (more on this in the next chapter) and development. This explains why some Generalists excel at big-picture thinking, others easily manage people, and still others quickly engender trust or confidently start a new project.

While the key attributes of curiosity, creative connections, and context function as the primary lens through which we understand our strengths, it is helpful to consider additional aspects that make each of us unique at work:

- **Freedom**: To use our particular strengths, many of us need specific types of freedom, such as freedom to engage in physical movement, question, connect with others, explore and test new ideas, research, and access outside information. Freedom also relates to how we adapt and can include exploring, changing course, thinking, experimenting, connecting, and more.

- **Learning**: As Generalists, we are characteristically deeply curious; how we learn differs based on our individual strengths. Types of learning can include being in conversation with others, learning through examination, experiential learning, active or independent reflection, research, and more.

- **Solo operator or team player**: Some of us prefer to work alone, others with a team, and many prefer a combination of both, where we need intervals of team and solo time.

- **Variability**: Generalists thrive on variability. The way variability is introduced or accessed can differ for each of us, depending on our strengths. Some individuals require variability in information, while others need it in people, their environment, and other aspects of their work.

- **Time/speed**: Some people need time to think and discern before deciding, while others thrive on deadlines or in a crisis. Even if people move quickly or more carefully, it's worth remembering that some decisions require more time, while others must be rapidly made, separate from preferences.

- **Process/goals**: Some people are motivated by the process (journey), while others are encouraged by the outcome (destination). Other people may be motivated by different factors, including vision, people, and context.

Strengths help crystallize curiosity

As described in the previous chapter, curiosity drives both how we learn and where our interests lie. As Generalists, we must understand the value of our shared attributes and how we interpret each individually. Strengths assist in doing precisely that.

Strengths help us understand the nuances of our curiosity. Do we enjoy getting to know people well and take time to form deep, meaningful relationships? Or do we easily and immediately understand the essence of someone at first introduction? Are we relentlessly curious about what is missing, and do we believe that once we know, everything will fall into place? Or do we love to collect information, knowing that it will be helpful to someone else in the future?

We also need to understand our process of acquiring, applying, and curating knowledge for both problems we want to address and those we do not yet know about. As Generalists, we often err on one side or the other, and acquire too much or not enough information. Both can be problematic. For example, Distracted Generalists, who risk becoming overly focused on details, benefit from understanding their learning process so they know when to pause and share their insights. Understanding our approach and learning patterns is one of the most potent insights we, as Generalists, can have to improve our performance and the problems we seek to solve.

The best way to learn who we are as Generalists is to learn from each other. The following case studies highlight how, as individuals, our strengths inform our particular type of curiosity.

CASE STUDY
A NEED FOR QUIET REFLECTION

Gemma grew up in a family of scientists who brought their powers of observation and questions to their parenting. On walks, they would pause and ask Gemma, "What do you see?" Starting simply enough, these conversations evolved into a series of increasingly complex questions and possible theories about what they saw, their origins, and purpose. This ability to observe and question served Gemma well in school, where she asked follow-up questions and was valued by her peers for her diplomacy and ability to see both sides of an argument. And yet Gemma struggled at her first professional job. Her role was conducting and summarizing research, which she enjoyed, yet she was repeatedly late in delivering her reports, which affected other people's work. Gemma tried to work more quickly but this turned into long hours and more mistakes. She became discouraged and didn't know what else she could do to improve her performance.

But then Gemma learned more about her strengths at a team retreat. She also received feedback from colleagues who appreciated her observant and thoughtful questions, but noted that she appeared quiet and uninterested when they began discussing different solutions as a team. The truth was that she found herself overwhelmed by the amount of information and her desire to understand it all. All she wanted was more time to really investigate the materials. Her strengths report explained why. Gemma had a strong desire to know every detail and a need for quiet time to process information, which, as she now understood, conflicted with the team's need to "think out loud" and decide quickly together.

In a conversation with her manager, she set a goal of "eighty percent done" as her "complete" version of specific tasks, enabling her to provide her colleagues with what they needed. She also asked that when a deeper dive was required on a research project, she be the one to do it. And finally, while the extensive team conversations were too chaotic for her to participate thoughtfully, she invited colleagues to connect with her for one-on-one discussions.

CASE STUDY
CURIOSITY AS CONNECTION

"Collecting people is my hobby," Lily explains before sharing her story that explains what she means.

Like her parents, Lily is wired for community. She built deep relationships while working at her family's restaurant, where she could satisfy both her curiosity about people and her ability to meet their needs quickly. She loved to be connected, both inside the restaurant and throughout every corner of her community. Yet not everyone in her family is as community-driven as Lily or sought to go into a similar business to her parents (in Lily's case, event planning). What drives her to be so curious about people?

It turns out that Lily has a combination of strengths that explains why she excels at creating and managing significant events. Lily brings to her work a deep sense of purpose, keen matchmaking abilities, and a love for momentum, which attracts attendees. One of Lily's superpowers is that her network lives inside her head. She easily remembers the names and interests of people she meets. When meeting someone for the first time, she immediately thinks about who else she knows that she should connect them to. Lily makes introductions based on shared purpose, not business.

Lily has turned her most natural strength into a thriving business. Now a consultant who advises organizations on large events, she uses her curiosity to animate experiences and grow an ever-expanding network of people who share her commitment to purpose and community.

What strengths support your "ranging curiosity"?

Strengths help foster creative connections

Whether we call it problem-solving, disparate connections, pattern identification, or connecting dots, Generalists seek solutions. As individuals, however, we are drawn to different kinds of challenges and bring distinct approaches, as explained in part by our strengths. For example, one Generalist may bring a hyper-focus on next steps, another may use a future framework to imagine what's possible, and yet another may look to the past to leverage what works. How we solve problems shows up in what we notice and the questions we ask.

The following case studies provide real-world examples of how Generalists who have identified their strengths understand and improve their ability to deliver needed solutions.

CASE STUDY
GAP FILLER TO SYSTEMS CONNECTOR

Chelsea's calm, measured demeanor belies an inquisitive and active mind. A valued senior leader in a medium-sized organization, Chelsea's longevity and the many roles she has filled make her a vital team member. There was no way for her to "move up" without becoming the CEO, a role that was neither open nor one she wanted. While she loved the organization, she was frustrated. She decided to explore her strengths and asked for her colleagues' feedback. They described her as stable, dependable, and holding institutional knowledge; unruffled, humble, and calm in a crisis.

While the feedback was flattering to Chelsea, it did not align with how she was feeling or the burden she carried of the team's dependence on her work. She was frustrated with carrying others' responsibilities and stymied by being internally focused. It seemed that every other day she had to step in and solve a new problem because no one else was available to do it. The internal demands highlighted her sense of disconnection to the larger non-profit world, where she had once been an active participant.

Chelsea's active reflection on her strengths, both in coaching conversations and guided writing, helped her realize the disconnect between her frustrations and how others perceived her. These insights also helped her shape a new direction for her work and the resulting conversations with the CEO. By moving away from being the "default" gap filler to a more strategic, outward and forward-facing role, she found what she had been missing: alignment, energy, and a renewed commitment to both purpose and work.

CASE STUDY
MORE THAN A NUMBER CRUNCHER

If you ask her colleagues, they all say they love Nadia for her positive energy. Feedback from team members, clients, and managers consistently describes her as the team cheerleader. A sympathetic ear and sound advice, especially on interpersonal issues, have further endeared her to the team. While positive, the feedback Nadia receives rarely pertains to her performance in her role.

Nadia is an accountant, a job she enjoyed until recently. Good at numbers, accounting seemed a secure career path to pursue after college. However, after a few years, she began to feel isolated and discouraged, and was spending too much time on the computer. She wanted more exposure to people and their challenges, but was unsure of what that would look like and fearful of taking the risk to find out.

Reflecting on her strengths assessment, she made the connection between her curiosity in people and how she found ways to make them feel included and hopeful, especially during challenging times such as the restructuring her company was undergoing. She had many examples of colleagues and friends trusting her advice. With this new understanding of why she likes "people problems," she became curious about how to support the team during change.

She discussed with her manager the prospect of expanding her role with an eye toward management, primarily through more strategic support. Her manager agreed, wanting Nadia to stay while immediately seeing the increased value she could bring. Together, they collaborated with the HR department and the outside consultant to integrate Nadia more intentionally into the team's change management processes. Nadia's creative approach helped her find a way to shift her focus, minimize risk, and, most importantly, support her team through the challenges ahead.

What strengths explain your lateral thinking and creative connections?

Strengths help define context

While we can apply our strengths to be curious and make creative connections, we must also seek environments where our strengths can be best supported. Understanding our strengths helps us recognize the context in which we can function most effectively, and, by extension, enables us to determine what we need from our managers, colleagues, and environment to excel.

While all Generalists need the freedom to be curious and think through creative solutions, we each have specific needs in our ideal environment. To be effective, some strengths require other people. For example, people who generate many possibilities to solve problems often need someone to bounce ideas off. Others might need quiet time to think and reflect before sharing their ideas with others.

The following case studies highlight how two different Generalists aligned their strengths with the proper working environment.

CASE STUDY
FROM THINK TANK TO START-UP

Elias likes to spend a lot of time walking the halls at work. On "in-office" days at his previous job, he came in and did a lap around the floor, greeting anyone and everyone before he settled into his own office. He would pop out again mid-morning and "take his walk," always stopping to talk to anyone who seemed available. While people appreciated Elias's friendly nature and warm greetings, some found his frequent visits disruptive.

Elias was well liked and successful, but he soon realized he was in the wrong environment. His need for connection, collaboration, and conversation—to spark ideas and solve problems—went unmet. While some folks were happy to engage, they did so as a favor to Elias, not because they valued the exchange. Aware of his need for freedom and, more importantly, problem-solving, Elias started looking for such an environment. He found a new role in a start-up based in an incubator space. The intimacy of the incubator provided exactly what Elias needed to thrive: a close connection with his team and the bonus of being in a space with other start-ups eager to communicate on mission and problem-solving.

CASE STUDY
CALM IN A CRISIS

Having completed her assessment and solicited feedback on her strengths, Teresa spent a few hours at a café, reading and reflecting on what she was learning about herself. There was agreement among colleagues that she was a little hard to get to know, though once you did get to know her, Teresa was very responsive to others' needs—especially in times of crisis. Her manager also deeply appreciated her attention to detail.

Teresa had loved her early professional office jobs. Still, after a few years in each role, she became bored and left. Eager to make another move, she wanted to be more intentional about where she was going. One of her favorite jobs was helping at events. She prevented problems by paying attention to every single detail. Short on a requested vegetarian dinner at a gala? She flagged the kitchen before the attendees even noticed. Speaker late? No worries—she had a backup video ready to roll.

Her calmness in a crisis was invaluable, as was her ability to ask the right questions and obtain answers easily, which enabled her to implement solutions more quickly. This new perspective helped Teresa think about the kinds of environments in which she thrived: dynamic, with many moving parts. With this insight, Teresa soon started a new role managing food service at a nearby university, she enjoyed the complexity of the daily food service, special events, and department lunches all across campus.

The process of who we are as Generalists is, by definition, ever evolving. Our curiosity drives us to question and learn constantly. Our interest in problems and opportunities ensures exploration and feedback. As we come to understand how our strengths describe who we are, we can, as Generalists, be clear about the value we bring to the gaps and needs we fill.

What types of environments and support help your strengths shine?

What's next?

The internal work of aligning our strengths with our abilities enables us to focus on the external work of communicating and collaborating with others, particularly with Specialists. Foundational to both is creating and building trust, which is essential to success, but challenging during times of change. In the next chapter, we will explore how Generalists can build trust, define key aspects of a narrative, and ultimately examine ways Generalists and Specialists can strengthen collaboration.

KEY POINTS

- Strengths serve Generalists in the same way skills serve Specialists; by defining their unique attributes and value in the absence of certifications, degrees, and so on.

- When we understand our strengths, we can further individualize Generalist attributes.

  - What talents support your ranging nature?

  - What talents support your connected thinking?

  - What do your talents need in terms of environment and support?

- Strengths help us identify our unique superpowers as a Generalist.

- Examples of other Generalists demonstrate the importance of knowing and using your strengths as a way to discern value and grow and thrive as a Generalist.

QUESTIONS FOR FURTHER REFLECTION

What kinds of strengths explain your adaptability and need for variability?

What does it feel like when you have an "aha" (aligned) moment?

How can you use your strengths intentionally to grow within the Development Framework?

WORKBOOK

See section 03 for
additional exercises.

5

CONFIDENCE, COMMUNICATION, AND COLLABORATION

"Great communication
begins with connection."

OPRAH WINFREY

WHEN WE FINALLY make sense of something about ourselves, we may struggle to share our new self-understanding with others. That moment of confidence and declaration—of trusting the words "I am…"—is often fleeting, as our mind quickly returns us to where we started: questioning, unsure, and now discouraged.

The irony, of course, is that if we want to be seen, heard, and understood, we can't expect others to read our minds or correctly guess our superpowers. Too often, we think we are alone, yet no one succeeds in isolation. By speaking up and sharing who we are and the value we bring, we can foster collaboration, demonstrate our dependability, and inspire trust—all while being seen and understood.

The bee and the spider

Just as Shakespeare's nickname ("jack-of-all-trades") captures the essence of Generalists, Jonathan Swift's 1704 satirical fable *The Battle of the Books*[34]—which contrasts the "Ancients" (Aristotle and Plato) and the "Moderns" (Descartes and Bacon)—captures the tension between Generalists and Specialists. In this story, a spider, signifying the Moderns, is the architect of a large, algorithmic web that ensnares a wandering bee, denoting the Ancients. The bee tears the delicate web, prompting the furiously spinning spider to name-call the bee a "vagabond" without a home or responsibility. The bee, unbothered by its meandering ways, responds philosophically: "Is beauty the spider's fragile web created from its bile or the honeycomb created from the wax and honey the bee has gathered far afield?"

The bee and spider's tense spat in 1704 could just as easily have been borrowed from a workplace conversation between a Specialist and a Generalist. Indeed, we could embrace the satire as something based on reality and end the story there. But what might happen if we lingered in this fable a little longer?

We could expect to find the spider and bee still in battle, arguing what—and by default, who—is "right." Yet in an updated version, perhaps we see the spider deep in architectural studies, meeting with other spiders to finesse the details of each other's complex web designs. The bee, binoculars in hand, flies about, scanning the changing landscape and finding ways to help the spider build a marvelous web, marshaling additional resources when needed. In this scenario, the spider trusts the bee's ability to look ahead, identify gaps, find new ways to think through a challenge, engage other Specialists, and mediate difficult moments. Likewise, the bee appreciates the spider's deep expertise and trusts its knowledge, only learning just enough to help develop a better, stronger, more flexible web. Together, through confidence, communication, and collaboration, their work exceeds anything they could have accomplished individually.

For better or worse, Swift's world of differing philosophies, abilities, and assumptions is familiar in today's work world. Disagreements on strategy, implementation, and interpersonal tensions contribute to employee disconnection, miscommunication, and disengagement. A 2024 Gallup report notes that thirty-two percent of American employees and twenty-six percent globally are disengaged, impacting the collaboration necessary to navigate the challenges of today's fast-paced world.[35] No one can achieve success alone, especially Generalists who need others to do what they do best: learn by asking questions, solve problems by testing ideas, and pilot solutions that create platforms for further specialization. Collaboration is possible when, like the spider and the bee, we find a shared sense of understanding. And as in every relationship, it begins with trust.

Confidence and trust

A key objective in this book is to help Generalists understand how to claim their value proposition confidently. With a definition, framework, and strengths-based approach, each of us can build toward an understanding of who we are as a Generalist. Confidence does more than help us discern and communicate our value; it changes how we see ourselves and how others see Generalists more broadly. Confidence requires that we commit to the value of what we bring (no longer defaulting to vague or confused descriptions) and the accountability that comes with commitment. It can be tricky to strike the right balance: too little confidence, and we begrudge the success of others and underdeliver on our potential; too much, and we can easily slide into arrogance.

A Generalist's confidence is built through intentional practice, reflection, and curiosity: we try, fail, learn, iterate, succeed, and start anew, knowing we can never know it all.

Yet there is something even more fundamental to confidence than practice: trust. Trust in ourselves, trust in processes, trust in others. Trust is often assumed, yet we rarely ask *why*. Why do we need trust, especially at work? According to *The Four Factors of Trust*, employees who trust are 260 percent more motivated at work, fifty percent less likely to look for other employment, and forty-one percent less likely to engage in absenteeism.[36]

Trust underpins both confidence and motivation, and is fostered by follow-through: doing what we say we will do. Trust, like many aspects of the work world, is trickier for Generalists than it is for Specialists. We know what Specialists do, and their qualifications, credentials, and years of stated expertise make Specialists initially easier to trust. Understandably, many people would doubt the knowledge and capacity of those who do not share a similar system of titles, credentialing, and stated expertise. After all, what does a jack-of-all-trades really know and do? Yet the ability to invite trust easily does not excuse Specialists from doing the work it takes to be trusted partners. Instead, it gives Generalists additional reasons to do so.

Trust serves an essential purpose in the relationship between Specialists and Generalists. Specialists need each other to learn and grow; Generalists need Specialists as both the reason and resource for our work. Trust is the foundational glue that elevates collaboration and expedites problem-solving. Though we may lack the titles and credentials that signal expertise, we can earn the trust of Specialists by sharing what we bring, how we learn, practice, and partner. Communicating our unique value and story of impact serves us better than "Trust me" ever will.

How do your strengths help you build trust?

Communication: creating a narrative

Common sense and key data support effective communication as the linchpin of trust. According to research published by Pumble, almost sixty percent of global employers say communication is the most desirable skill in job applicants.[37] Meanwhile, a 2021 McKinsey study on the future of work reports that employees included in effective workplace communication are almost five times more likely to report increased productivity.[38] And yet, as Generalists, we can easily confuse trust and communication with intention and action, instead believing that our work speaks for itself, evident to everyone we work with. Who needs qualifications when we can figure it out for ourselves? We are relentlessly curious! We solve problems for fun! We can get it done! And we do and have done. Yet, our efforts, without intention and effective communication, can be disruptive and discouraging to people and processes.

As Generalists, we have agency and voice; we can flip the script from assuming our actions alone communicate our value. We can choose to build trust and signal effectiveness through our unique story. We can tell, not just show, the story of how we work and the difference we make to both engender and build trust.

In short, we can create our Generalist narrative.

Discerning our own story as a Generalist might be the most challenging part of our efforts to become a Mature Generalist, rooted in strengths, owning our abilities, and being adaptive to the challenges around us. No one sees themselves objectively; we all struggle between a desired image and one that is authentic, more vulnerable, and even flawed. We are also challenged by wanting to be all things to all people, yet, as we have undoubtedly learned time and again, when we are "everything to everyone," we lose control of our story and definition, risking our value and agency.

How do you explain your impact?

A narrative is *your* story. It must convey *your* value in a way that gives the listener, reader, hiring manager, or anyone else insight into who *you* are. At its best, a narrative paints an immediate and deft picture of who we are, where we fit in, and, with retelling, deepens our value proposition, trust, and collaboration. To evoke this picture, our story must grab attention and be easily understood.

How do we figure out our narrative? We begin by examining the longer backstory of our career, identifying key themes, twists, and turns. With effort and often with a coach, we use the backstory to distill a concise value proposition, highlighting what we bring and the impact we have, and then refine even further to find language that hooks our audience or "pops" in other communications and channels. A successful narrative answers three key questions:

- **What do we *bring*?** When we are specific about what we each carry as Generalists, we give the kind of information Specialists communicate through title and credentials. This includes the unique ways in which we learn, think, develop relationships, communicate, influence, and do work. Our work successes and frustrations, as well as colleague and client feedback, give insight into how our strengths manifest in our work. It's also essential to identify what we *don't bring*, allowing for a deeper understanding of our value and story.

- **When and *where* do we thrive?** In addition to a nuanced understanding of our ideal work environment, it is essential to identify the specific work we excel at. This includes the problems we like to tackle, the kinds of teams in which we succeed, and the conditions in which we flourish.

- **What *impact* do we have?** While we live in a world where success is hyper-individualized, it is rarely, if ever, a solo act. While Specialists can often point to specific contributions as evidence of success, Generalists have a harder time claiming impact. We are not the scientists who made the discovery, the chefs who created the menu, the doctors who completed the surgery, or the candidates who won the race. Yet when we do use language that precisely describes our contribution to the collective, we can map our efforts to personal success. Language is essential here: words that signal connection, contribution, and a focus on collective capacity can paint a detailed picture of impact that we lack the metrics to capture.

Successful Generalist narratives

While each narrative is unique, examples of Generalists who have claimed their narrative can give us a model for developing our own story. Each case study featured here refers to the iterative process that results in a Generalist narrative that rings authentic and true.

CASE STUDY
THE IMPOSTOR SPECIALIST

As Generalists, we share the experience of either seeking or defaulting to a Specialist role and consequently struggling with our limitations in the role. We discover that at some point, we lack a Specialist's focus or expertise, yet still cling to a definition of a Specialist's career and success instead of figuring out our own. Gary found himself in this exact scenario, faced with the challenge of abandoning his former identity as a serial Specialist to embrace his deeper value as a Generalist.

Gary is, by any definition, intelligent and curious. His dry sense of humor and desire to be helpful are greatly appreciated by the people he works with. For years, Gary successfully translated complex tech-talk into clear, doable actions for team members. He was also valued by sales teams for the same ability, helping to translate the same tech-talk into client pro-posals and support.

After leaving his last company, he achieved success as a solo consultant and, driven by curiosity and emerging technology, delved into data analytics. After a few years, he missed working in a team environment and was unsuccessful in securing several data analyst roles. He doubled down and decided to complete a third master's degree in data analytics. Still no luck. Discouraged, Gary began to doubt his abilities. How had he thrived in complex tech companies before, yet now, even with a master's in the subject, could not get an interview?

One challenge was that Gary's interest and degree in data analytics did not help him successfully compete against data analysts, many of whom were younger. Additionally, his resume did not adequately highlight his experience with data analysis. To go back in-house, Gary needed to highlight his appreciation and use of data by connecting it to his past successes. The question for Gary was: What did he bring to a future team beyond his ability to learn about new (data) trends?

As part of developing his narrative, Gary reflected on past jobs and the people he most enjoyed working with. All three happened to be his managers and shared key qualities: they were all big thinkers, generous with information, welcomed feedback, and shared a sense of humor. These managers did not hire Gary for his expertise in technology. They hired him for his strengths in relating to teams and to help them translate the abstract into action. By investigating his successes through a "team lens," not a skills lens, Gary distilled the essential themes of his narrative. He was able to settle on a shorter value proposition by taking the perspective of his former managers.

Gary started with a cv that signaled specialization and data analytics to a more honest and aligned narrative: a "translator of vision into action, managing teams through testing and improving solutions for systemic problems." Gary now leads with the idea of a "translator to address complex solutions," which changes both how he discusses his value proposition and his target audience. Once focused on reaching out to researchers seeking data analysts, he now looks for leaders in need of someone who can translate vision into data-supported action.

CASE STUDY
ONE COMPANY, EVERY ROLE

While many Generalists move frequently from one company to the next, some spend a chunk of time in one organization. They are hired, achieve success, and then are asked to fill another role elsewhere in the company. These Generalists are deeply valued for their company knowledge, yet, like Generalists everywhere, they often struggle to understand their value. While Samuel had many years of experience in his company, he would usually ask himself: How can I capture my value across my many roles?

Samuel has been at the same company for what feels like forever when compared with many of his colleagues. He has been working with the CEO in some capacity since the company was founded around a kitchen table. It soon expanded to a shared office, grew further into its office suites, expanded nationally, survived the COVID pandemic, and now operates as a hybrid model with staff spread across the country, convening a few times a year for in-person learning and connection.

Samuel was at an inflection point in his own life: his kids were now in college, and he had more time, freedom, and mental space to explore new opportunities outside the company. While grateful for his many roles and opportunities at work, Samuel recognized that his work history did not align with a traditional resume. A known quantity within his company, he had never even needed an introduction. The CEO just called him up and deployed him where needed. But outside the company? It was an entirely different—and new—story.

Samuel had to think about how to address the challenge of writing his resume in a way that made sense externally. He began by writing a description of each role he held at the company, including the title, the reason for his assignment, his achievements in each role, and the reasons for his transfer to the next role or project. He also went on something of a "listening tour," asking those he had worked with for feedback, and was surprised to discover how many of his colleagues said he was a "quick thinker," "easy to work with," and "calm."

Through that process and working with a coach, Samuel realized that most of his work involved being something of a trusted extension of the CEO, focusing on emerging and strategic needs. While he had many "interim" titles, his reading convinced him he was somewhere between a chief of staff and an in-house strategist. Samuel's process culminated in a value proposition that positioned him as a "strategic adviser helping teams build trust by working on 'what's next'." This short sentence (with an appropriate example included) was enough for him to use in networking conversations. He soon transitioned to a part-time role working on behalf of the CEO and several outside projects with new clients.

CASE STUDY
NO WINS, NO WAY UP

Most Generalists struggle to communicate how their work creates clear outcomes. Generalists often play the essential role in coordinating a team, catalyzing a project, collaborating across departments, and even working behind the scenes to smooth over interpersonal grievances, client complaints, or mercurial leaders. In every instance, Generalists ensure progress can proceed. Yet when it comes to claiming wins—units sold, people managed, and KPIs met—Generalists like Nicolette, who work within and across teams, struggle with how to "own" their successes. If everything Nicolette does is in support of or with others, how can she communicate her role in shared success?

Nicolette is a project associate at a tech company of just under 100 employees. Based on feedback from team members and her reflections, she recognizes that her unique strengths include enthusiasm, positivity, and action. She was not surprised by this, as colleagues from the school where she had taught previously had said as much. She left the school nearly three years ago and pivoted to being a project associate supporting several teams. Eager to be promoted, she recognizes the need to convey her value beyond mere "feel-good" aspects to her manager and colleagues within the company.

Looking at her past successes through the lens of her superpowers, Nicolette felt most aligned when she was in the trenches, working side-by-side to solve complex problems in a way that turned colleagues into lifelong friends. She could explain part of her value by showing how she contributed to solving problems, but she still struggled with how to relate her work to the ever-important bottom line that mattered to her manager. She wasn't the team manager, so she couldn't claim a leadership role, nor was she an engineer or an expert on the relevant issues. She realized, however, that on the teams she actively supported, no one left the team. It wasn't what she did but what she prevented that could serve as a relevant data point.

In addition to retention, several senior engineers had asked her to join their teams because her can-do attitude made hitting deadlines almost fun. She incorporated their requests, the retention data, and her insights into a draft that she could build upon when discussing her value to her manager. While Nicolette initially resisted claiming success, sharing the specific ways she positively influenced team dynamics and likely retained team members allowed her to claim not just impact, but outcomes.

CASE STUDY
ALIGNING VALUE AND VALUES

Not every work environment suits every Generalist. But knowing a company's values can help Generalists determine whether they will thrive in that environment. This is what happened to Stephanie. She struggled at work until she asked herself: How does my value proposition align with the company's values and culture?

Stephanie worked at a nonprofit before she left for a higher salary and new challenges as a manager in the learning and development team at a larger company. Just after graduation, Stephanie had worked with a coach to pinpoint what she cared about, including her genuine desire to care for humankind and her interest in helping people reach their full potential. While she excelled in her role and enjoyed the team at this larger company, Stephanie felt that she wasn't living her values, where revenue equaled impact.

She decided to ask her colleagues what they valued about the company. Everyone she spoke to felt supported by the company's explicit value of improving the lives of employees, even if they didn't talk about it as a mission in the same way the nonprofit did. With this new perspective, Stephanie began to see how this related to her work of helping colleagues learn and grow. At the request of her manager, Stephanie drafted a statement to serve as her guiding principle, and to share with other colleagues when first meeting them as a means to develop the trust she needed to be successful in her role. The statement read: "I make our company commitment to doing the best by people real by helping teams learn and grow."

Collaboration: working with Specialists

Understanding how we continuously reinforce trust through sharing our story also helps us build muscle for successful partnerships. For Generalists, successful collaboration is predicated on our ability to learn, solve problems, and be effective partners in practice with Specialists.

WAYS A GENERALIST CAN HELP SPECIALISTS

- Get curious about their work and stay connected to its evolution.

- Know enough to appreciate, connect, and act on information; there's no need to "be" the Specialist.

- Seek out solutions that include Specialist insights.

- Communicate clearly when you're thinking versus doing; if you're offering an idea, say so. When asking someone to do something, be clear and concise in your request.

- Communicate your role in the collaboration. Think about your narrative and how it applies in this instance.

- Be sure to share preferences for receiving feedback on your particular Generalist strengths and other skills, and ask others about their approach.

- Understand what motivates the Specialists on your team.

- Be sure to confirm the shared vision and goal, especially when challenges arise.

- Know how teammates want support and feedback.

WAYS SPECIALISTS CAN SUPPORT A GENERALIST

- Recognize their value as a Generalist and not a "subpar" or impostor Specialist.

- Share their knowledge with a focus on right-sized information. Be available for questions, even if they seem elementary.

- Depend on Generalists to share their big-picture observations.

- Seek Generalists out as "what if" partners for new ways to think through a problem.

- Support Generalists who are connecting across silos and building bridges.

- Stay focused on contribution as a Specialist.

- Manage outreach to other Specialists.

- Share credit.

How do you collaborate, and what could it be going forward?

So, what does effective collaboration for Generalists look like? In addition to project management, effective feedback processes, and other systems, as Generalists we need to be able to both lead and support collaboration that builds upon trust and value. The guidelines that help Generalists successfully collaborate can be used by anyone, and can even be used as a template for launching successful projects. They include:

- **Preparation**: Any collaboration, whether with two people or many more, can start with a "kick-off" where preferred work style, needs, strengths, and expectations are shared before engaging in the actual work. Taking the time to clarify roles, and understand the particulars of individual work styles and preferences for feedback ensures effective communication and conflict resolution. Generalists can initiate and lead these conversations as one way to convey value in a collaboration.

- **Playing to our strengths**: This is obvious but worth restating: as Generalists, we need to play to our strengths as practitioners. While tempting, we must resist approximating a Specialist instead of complementing their expertise. By seeking to understand how each team member shows up, Generalists can better leverage collective strengths in service of the best solution. Additionally, a shared language based on strengths creates greater awareness and collaboration.

- **Navigating bumps**: Any change, process, or growth includes bumps along the way. These challenging moments are vital for Generalists to be, again, "practitioners" and lead with curiosity. Knowing how to give and receive effective feedback—the kind that helps us move forward and grow—is essential when navigating bumps. Agreeing on how to deal with conflict and unexpected challenges can start with asking those involved what questions need to be asked and how a learning mindset can be supported. (More on effective feedback in Chapter 7.)

- **Sharing success**: For Generalists, shared success is also our success, so we must be specific about how we contribute, regardless of any particular title we have or role we fill. Did you catalyze the project, or serve as convener, facilitator, or manager? Did you contribute to strategy, partnerships, process, or delivery? What part of the work would not have happened if you had not been involved? Where did you make a specific difference? For example, was there a problem ahead that you recognized and addressed before others noticed? Did you smooth over ruffled feathers or facilitate collaborations that no one else thought to? Did you champion or cheerlead others so they felt connected to the work?

CASE STUDY
AN ENVIRONMENT WHERE SPECIALISTS AND GENERALISTS SUCCEED

Hospitals provide a good example of where Specialists and Generalists succeed. In the service of patients, they work together to solve various problems and improve effectiveness.

Titles confer the roles and level of expertise in just about every organization with any hierarchy, hospitals included. And yet those in a hospital know, perhaps better than anyone else, that no one role succeeds without the others. Everyone is part of a team—and collaboration with others, inside and outside the operating room, can be a matter of life and death. Many of the people who work in a hospital are Specialists, as indicated by their titles and responsibilities, and include anesthesiologists, ER nurses, the administrators who handle billing, and patient assistants who perform various tasks. Each has a specific role to play in a patient's successful outcome.

However, specialization in a hospital requires making way for a Generalist. In this case, the Hospitalist. Hospitalists do not specialize in one area of medicine, but instead serve as an "in-hospital" general doctor for patients with complex health issues and who have many specialists. Their responsibility is to take into account existing health issues that may complicate surgery or recovery. There are others in the hospital too, who, by nature and function, work across an organization, a project, or a team, and fill gaps by providing solutions that, in many cases, support the work of Specialists. This includes the CEO, the chief of staff, the entrepreneurs who created the technology within the hospital, the project managers who assisted with the artificial joints, and, occasionally, the marketing lead or consultant who helped in this department or with the adoption of best practices.[39]

As Generalists, our work means we can never "win" alone. When we take the time to build trust, we exceed even our expectations, with stronger work relationships, better learning habits, the capacity to manage risk, and much more.

What's next?

Having spent time exploring how we build confidence, communication, and collaboration, in Chapter 6 we will turn our focus to how we develop a career as a Generalist. While there are many successful Generalists in wildly different settings, we will explore various models, likely roles, and the impact of environment (and all aspects of context) on developing a Generalist career. In Chapter 7, we will address self-management, development, and growth.

KEY POINTS

- Generalists must recognize and trust their unique abilities to effectively build confidence, communicate, and collaborate with others, particularly Specialists.

- A successful partnership is predicated on successful communication, which Generalists can help facilitate, in part by creating a Generalist narrative.

- Narratives are stories; their core remains the same, but they are adapted to meet audience needs and evolve.

- Collaboration is essential to Generalists' success: we need Specialists to do our work.

- Effective collaboration with Generalists requires more from Generalists in terms of communication and clarification of roles.

QUESTIONS FOR FURTHER REFLECTION

What in these case studies can you relate to and borrow from?

_____

_____

_____

What do your different audiences (clients, colleagues, hiring managers, etc.) need to know about your work and impact?

_____

_____

_____

What are some ways you can communicate your value proposition that feel authentic and help you embrace Mature Generalist abilities?

_____

_____

_____

WORKBOOK

See section 05 for
additional exercises.

6

THE GENERALIST CAREER

"Do not go where the path
may lead, go instead where there
is no path and leave a trail."

RALPH WALDO EMERSON

UNDERSTANDING OUR GENERALIST value may seem enough for us to proceed with a satisfying and successful career. It is not. We have identified our unique superpowers and are now using them to shape our careers. This might seem complicated given that Generalists are inherently adaptive: how can one plan for a job if you thrive in change? And it's true—a traditional career model, including the credentials and competencies that define Specialists, does not work well for Generalists. But just as we lacked a definition, we do not have to default to what is missing when we have a framework that can fulfill what we need. Just as in other aspects of the Generalist journey, there are alternative career models and roles that provide us with opportunities to succeed as practitioners, and adapt to the change around us.

Faulty career models

As Generalists, we take on roles that pique our curiosity and offer a chance to learn and grow, only to soon find out that they are not a good fit. While we can self-direct other attributes, context is necessarily external to our control and requires discernment. We cannot control the environment and conditions in which we work. Yet, it is often the make-or-break of our success, and responsible for the big hits and even bigger misses that characterize a Generalist's zigzag career.

The unpredictable ups and downs of a "default" Generalist career can feel like a roller coaster with no destination. Milly Tamati, founder of Generalist World, and other Generalists use the term "spiky career" to describe their work journey. Borrowed from the neurodivergent world, "spiky" represents an extreme variability of skills. For Generalists, a spiky career's peaks are the successes that happen when talents align with opportunity. The lows can be for several reasons: trying and falling short of "being" a Specialist; misalignment in culture, expectations, skills, or roles; and the creep of boredom and "job hopping." While the "highs" of a spiky career confirm our value and can feel wonderful, the lows are disproportionately more damaging. As reported by O.C. Tanner, when surveyed, fifty-six percent of Generalists don't believe they have a clear career, and thirty-five percent feel excluded from promotions.[40] And if the damage to both confidence and bank account is not enough, the spiky career fails to develop the talents we need as Generalists.

Spiky Career

Coach

Start-Up

Start-Up

Teacher

Vice President

Foundation

Start-Up

Corporation

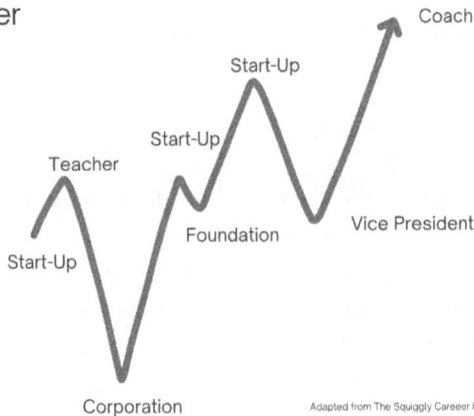

Adapted from The Squiggly Career by Helen Tupper and Sarah Ellis

Like the spiky career, the mid-career squeeze is similarly frequent and discouraging for Generalists, especially in professional service industries and consulting. The mid-career squeeze can be envisioned as an hourglass, which starts and ends with Generalist-satisfying opportunities, and has a hard-to-navigate Specialist squeeze in the middle.

The Hourglass-shaped Model of Career Change

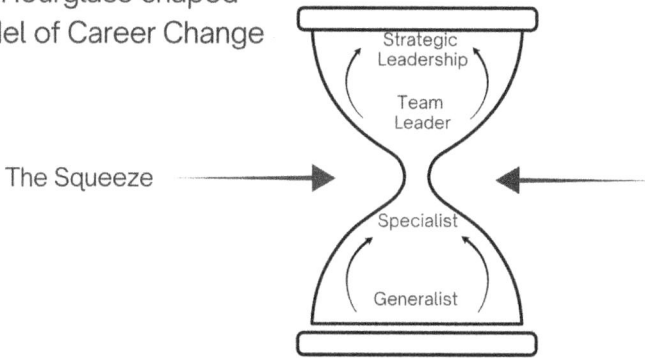

The Squeeze

Strategic Leadership

Team Leader

Specialist

Generalist

Adapted from John Adair "100 Greatest Ideas for Effective Leadership"

Source: John Adair41

Those who experience this squeeze might, for example, start their career at a consulting firm and learn every aspect of the business. They thrive as an associate, successfully navigating the variability of tasks, roles, and projects. Yet, to advance, they must specialize and choose an industry or marketable area of expertise. This is the beginning of the squeeze. Then, once they have been an expert for a while, they may again expand into a senior role with strategic, management, and operational responsibilities. The factors that made the Generalist associate successful explain their success in the C-suite. Yet getting through the squeeze, which requires different skills to be successful, is neither easy nor always possible, and is often the time when people leave a company.

"People may spend their whole lives
climbing the ladder of success only to find,
once they reach the top, that the ladder
is leaning against the wrong wall."

THOMAS MERTON

As defaults, the spiky and squeeze models offer little to Generalists. More often they are detrimental, leading to confusion, self-doubt, and, with frequent job changes and gaps between employment, negative impacts on earnings and promotions for many General-ists.[42] Fortunately, newer models are available that better align with the needs of building a successful career as a Generalist.

Three new(ish) career models

For the first time in history, there are five generations in the work-place, each with a unique perspective, experience, and challenges. The careers of Boomers (born between 1946 and 1964) typically align with specialization and the traditional career ladder; a clear role and progress "up" a ladder of increasing responsibility, salary, and reputation. Younger Millennials (1981–1996) and Generation Z (1997–2012) differ significantly from Boomers. They care more about their quality of life, mental health, and the impact of stress— and therefore are more inclined to quit a job that doesn't align with their lifestyle. They also seek career advice from social media, with over fifty percent using AI tools and platforms such as TikTok.[43] Generation Z, raised in the information age, is already wired to adapt to rapid changes in the work world.

A multi-generational workforce has transformed work culture, prompting employers to adapt to employee demands and seek more inclusive, value-driven approaches. Leaders and managers are addressing burnout by promoting well-being and offering a variety of hybrid work options and development opportunities. These changes uniquely benefit Generalists of all generations, creating space for new approaches to career development.

Enter: the squiggle, portfolio, and fractional career models.

In late 1990, Michael Driver, a professor at the Marshall School of Business at the University of Southern California, identified four preferred career concepts.[44] The first two are familiar: linear, the classic "moving up the corporate ladder" model; and expert, "being the best." The other two models identified by Driver are of interest to Generalists: a "spiral career" is defined by moving laterally from one position to a related position every five to ten years. In contrast, the "roamer career" is characterized by frequent changing between unrelated jobs.

Squiggly Career

Finish school · Get a job · Finish program · Change occupations · Choose a program · Go back and finish program · Change jobs · Change programs · Take a year off · Go back to school · Work part-time · Fractional role

The Squiggly Career by Helen Tupper and Sarah Ellis

In many ways, Driver anticipated "the squiggly career,"[45] the topic and title of a 2020 bestselling book in the UK. Helen Tupper and Sarah Ellis were unlikely university friends, yet they shared similar career paths that were more of a "squiggle" than a traditional ladder. Their book, popular TED Talk, and podcast demystify the process of intentionally transitioning from one career to another. They recognize that the days of "one career and one job" are long gone, and everyone now has the opportunity to design a career—and a squiggle—that can be successful despite traditional norms.

For Generalists, a squiggle career is a logical career. It mirrors the way we think and do our work; moving from one role to another satisfies our need for variability and activates our curiosity and learning. The squiggle career, as described by Tupper and Ellis, is created with care and intention. Understanding one's strengths, interests, and passions can allow individuals to develop a plan to move from one career to another. Courses, side gigs, apprenticeships, and other avenues enable people to test and build their new career before committing fully.

Portfolio Career

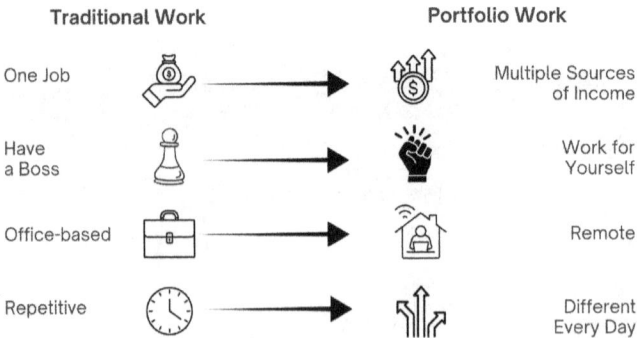

Traditional Work				Portfolio Work
One Job		→		Multiple Sources of Income
Have a Boss		→		Work for Yourself
Office-based		→		Remote
Repetitive		→		Different Every Day

@ThePortfolioCollective

Christina Wallace, author of *The Portfolio Life*,[46] is, like Tupper and Ellis, calling attention to non-linear careers. Wallace, an associate professor at Harvard, writes about portfolio careers that feature concurrent, rather than sequential, careers. Typically, people with portfolio careers have several areas of interest or capability. They might manage a health-tech incubator for new companies, consult for other start-ups, and teach business students. A single Generalist could be a fractional CIO for an early-stage entrepreneur for fifteen hours a week, manage a website and bookings part-time for several rental properties, and even have a "side gig" producing and selling candles on Etsy. To some, this may appear random and even haphazard, yet a portfolio approach allows Generalists to pursue concurrent careers that cater to their multiple talents, interests, and need for variety.

Career Models

	Fractional	Consultant	Part-time
Scope	High-level strategic and leadership	Specialized expertise for a discrete project	Focus on day-to-day or project work
Time	Embedded from 6m+ to 2 years	Short-term, defined timeline	Set number of hours per week/month
Integration	Function as exec. team member	External, independent advisor	Less embedded
Compensation	Pro-rate fraction of FT salary	Paid per project, hourly or retainer	Paid hourly or per project
Focus	Long-term impact and outcomes	Complete specified task or deliverable	Execute on daily tasks and projects

Adapted from "What is a Fractional Role" from teamlfied.co.

What career models resonate and why?

A third approach, one with increasing popularity, is a "fractional" role. Fractional roles are strategic roles and, unlike a consultant, have leadership and decision-making responsibilities. Generalists with fractional roles perform the same function for multiple companies. For example, a CFO may support three different clients. Fractional work has grown significantly in popularity, with the Bureau of Labor reporting an increase of eighteen percent from 2021 to 2022 and a fifty-seven percent rise since 2020.[47] Driven in part by hiring constraints, this trend underscores the cost-effectiveness of fractional talent and interim support. Similar to the portfolio approach, fractional work is an increasingly popular option that offers employers a flexible and cost-effective staffing solution, with the added benefit of increased productivity. For Generalists, fractional work satisfies our need for variety with a diverse range of clients.

The squiggle, portfolio, and fractional models all offer Generalists career templates that align with our adaptability and attributes. All three models allow for near-term planning and longer-term evolution, thereby smoothing out the lows and perpetuating the highs that often occur in "spiky" careers. But like everything a Generalist encounters, how we adapt and thrive is what matters.

Operating environment

As discussed in Chapter 3, the context or operating environment in which Generalists can best express their abilities will vary from one individual to the next. Context comprises many factors, including the type of industry, company size, stage, office environment, role (to be discussed in the next section), and, vitally, culture. Some of us thrive in a start-up, while others enjoy working in larger corporations, and still others prefer to be external and work as consultants. Factors to consider include:

- **Size**: While the definition can change by industry and type, the US Small Business Administration defines a small business as having fewer than 500 employees. However, a small start-up company may have ten to fifty people and consider an IPO when it reaches 300 to 400 employees. Company size influences Generalist opportunities. Small companies and start-ups often depend on a team of Generalists who can adapt to meet the many demands of building a new company without having to rely on Specialists (who are usually hired later in the growth process). In a larger organization, a Generalist can be particularly effective working between teams of Specialists, developing strategy, and addressing gaps.

- **Scale and transition**: The stage and pace of growth or change are related to an organization's size. Whether an organization is on an aggressive growth path (scaling) or navigating change (transition), Generalists can find opportunities to thrive. Start-ups often scale and transition from one stage of growth to another fairly quickly, frequently offering Generalists new opportunities. At larger corporations where change may be slower, there are in-house opportunities related to innovation, change, and growth. Generalists can meet short-term staffing needs, participate in or lead strategic, business, and operational planning, onboard and manage new staff, and test and pilot new ideas and initiatives.

- **Culture and environment**: Company culture can be the make-or-break factor for any employee, including Generalists. Many factors contribute to culture, including stated and practiced values, leadership, management effectiveness, and overall employee engagement. While every individual will have a different set of values and needs in terms of an effective operating culture, Generalists share a need for a certain level of freedom to learn, explore, connect, and practice. Other factors related to culture include the physical space and whether work is in-person, hybrid, or fully remote. Other factors to consider include employee satisfaction (especially that of other Generalists), performance philosophy and measures (for Specialists and others), opportunities for in-house growth and development, and access to mentors, programs, or externally available learning opportunities.

- **Leadership and management**: Like culture, leadership and management significantly influence an individual's work world. Generalists require leaders who possess a clear vision, an understanding of their needs, and a willingness to allow experimentation and practice, all of which are essential for meeting the demands of change. The role of the manager is vital for Generalists. Gallup reports that fifty-two percent of exiting employees say their supervisor or organization could have done something to prevent them from leaving their job.[48] Generalists need managers who understand them for who they are and do not compare or give feedback on their work, performance, or development as if they were Specialists. Managers who individualize their expectations and assessments to align with a Generalist's strengths and needed competencies can be the game-changer for us to have a long-term, prosperous career.

As highlighted in the following case study, the environment in which you operate as a Generalist can have a significant impact on your work satisfaction and success.

CASE STUDY
TRIAL AND ERROR

Katherine is the first to tell you that her success at work is due to two fundamental lessons she learned as a goalie on a Division 1 team. Lesson one: Team first. Self-promotion is a barrier to what is best for team success, leadership included. Lesson two: Take a wide view. As a goalkeeper, Katherine learned the value of assessing the field and identifying gaps where she can step in and help others.

Curious about tech and early-stage companies, Katherine left a large corporation for a relatively new start-up. Excited about the vision, culture, and growth stage, she was attracted to the idea that expansion could have even more impact. However, an unexpected setback in funding led to a rapid reallocation and relocation of staff, rather than managing a team expansion. This change required careful planning within a short time frame and involved layoffs, transfer offers, and numerous role reassignments for the 120 employees.

Despite the circumstances, laid-off employees gave a favorable review of the experience. Katherine, however, felt that leadership lacked the team-first approach she valued. She disagreed with some of the decisions and realized she would have managed the process quite differently. Unlike at her previous job, Katherine realized that no one on the current leadership team had ever played a Division 1 sport, and so did not understand—and nor did she communicate—her perspective. Discouraged and disincentivized, Katherine chose to hire her replacement (team first) before her amicable departure from the company. A month later, she reflected on her journey and next step. If not within a corporation or a start-up, where did she belong?

Katherine's experience in a start-up was challenging for several reasons: the role itself was not a good fit, as she could not leverage her strengths, and she did not align with the senior team's values. This was the first time Katherine had left a role discouraged and disappointed, and her confidence took a hit. She began to doubt whether she could find a "next step," and thought she might have to take a "step back" to find her way in the kind of culture she now knew she needed to thrive. Taking the time to discern her value and ground in her experiences brought her to a larger, more developed organization looking to scale. She is now in a role that allows her to experience what it takes to scale, but within a larger corporate setting and a senior leadership team that includes former D1 athletes, who share her team-first value.

Roles and responsibilities

In addition to the physical environment, role and responsibilities play a part in context. As Generalists, we are familiar with the experience of scrolling through job postings, finding opportunities we know we could excel in, yet our lack of "required" experience (and the screening used by recruiters) makes us reconsider whether we should even apply. And when we do apply, we must discern fit and make a convincing case. That said, there are three general categories of roles that Generalists can consider: managerial roles, in which Generalists typically excel; a Generalist version of a Specialist role; and an entrepreneurial role.

Managerial roles

The work of other people is the work of a Generalist; our necessary experience as collaborators gives us early exposure to the role and efficacy of a manager. As Generalists, our curiosity and ability to see gaps across an organization make us particularly effective managers of people, processes, and/or projects.

For many Generalists, it is our curiosity in people that explains why many, but certainly not all, Generalists find themselves in managerial or other "people" roles. If we have strengths that relate to people (the "essential skills"), we are motivated to help others be their best and have a commitment to their development and growth. Some Generalists understand how individuals can excel in different roles, whereas others may be particularly effective at bringing together a team to test new approaches. In addition to aligning with their particular strengths, the Generalist's need for variability in opportunities and dynamics is often met by the demands of being a good manager. However, if the role of management is to maintain consistency and accuracy rather than adapt and evolve, the Generalist will likely fail.

Describe the attributes of the best managers you have had; how did they invest in developing your abilities?

There are three types of management. Consider each as a lens through which we can align our strengths with the different responsibilities of each:

- **People management**: Generalists who are relational in their approach and have a curiosity about people can excel at building and managing teams by, for example, aligning individual talents with roles and finding authentic ways to boost and maintain high morale. They may also be effective in helping siloed teams resolve tensions, reconnect, and find ways to collaborate more effectively. A people manager's work is fundamentally about the work and growth of others, and their impact is often measured by overall team performance.

- **Project management**: Generalists who notice information gaps and enjoy connecting the dots are often effective at managing the disparate parts, pieces, and people that make up a project. Generalists who are particularly adept at starting and building may excel at figuring out the path forward or easily adapting the process to changing conditions. The limited time frame of many projects is also appealing to Generalists: project managers will often collaborate with individuals for short periods—in groups, individually, or in sequence. While managing people is part of project management, they do not have responsibility for development and growth, and may give input rather than be responsible for team performance.

- **Process management**: Creating processes (or systems) is essential to any initial efforts at growth. Process management differs from project or product management in that it is focused on a specific need or improvement and is time-limited: the Generalist does not go on to manage what their contribution is. For example, a Generalist may help manage the hiring process, both finding people and finding more efficient ways to address what can be improved. A manager focused on process will, like a project manager, engage with individuals and teams, often sequentially and iteratively, but not have development or managerial responsibilities.

Specific roles in which Generalists typically thrive

In addition to the different kinds of management discussed above, there are specific roles in which Generalists typically thrive based on an alignment of strengths and experience. Roles such as COO, chief of staff, and consultant are often well-suited for Generalists, as are roles that focus on strategy or improving effectiveness. Brief descriptions of roles frequently (but not always) occupied by Generalists include:

- **CEO**: According to a 2018 *Harvard Business Review* article titled "The Fastest Path to the CEO Job," ninety percent of the 17,000 CEOs surveyed over ten years had previous Generalist experience.[49] Whether it is the entrepreneur (founder) or someone who has risen through the ranks, the CEO role demands many of the attributes that Mature Generalists in particular readily bring. The CEO establishes vision, direction, and priorities, making decisions and inspiring confidence in employees. A Generalist's ability to range across issues, trends, and departments to discern a path forward is beneficial in a CEO role.

- **COO**: A COO is responsible for the operations of a company, ensuring that the day-to-day business runs smoothly across all departments, including finance, HR, administration, and any client or customer service. Internally, the COO collaborates and implements strategy, aligns organizational goals with performance expectations, identifies strategies to manage risk, and models culture. The COO serves on the leadership team and reports to the CEO. Mature Generalists who have had exposure to, and previous responsibilities in several of the functions—for example, HR, administration, and perhaps finance—can thrive as a COO working across the organization to align internal workings with external efforts.

- **Chief of staff**: This role supports the CEO or a department lead and serves, in many ways, as their "right hand and left brain." A CoS is a very personal hire, and the job description changes based on who the CEO is and what they need. But every CoS operates as an extension of their CEO and may lead strategic projects, communicate on behalf of the CEO, and serve as a key advisor. The CEO's administrative support resides with an executive assistant. Like the COO, the CoS helps with internal effectiveness.

- **Strategy**: The function of strategy can be fulfilled in several roles, both internally and externally, as a consultant. At larger companies, there may be a chief strategy officer and a director or manager of strategy. At smaller organizations, the COO or chief of staff may be responsible for strategy, while the CEO or external consultants might be used to help determine strategic direction. Generalists who enjoy solving problems excel in strategic roles where they can pursue what's next, engage with stakeholders, and identify multiple recommendations.

- **Product/program management**: As previously mentioned, product and program management roles typically encompass responsibilities for product or program development, delivery, improvement, evaluation, and revenue generation. The scope of duties leverages Generalists' adaptability and need for variability.

- **Partner/client management**: Similar to program management, these roles leverage Generalists' attributes and also offer variability, especially to Generalists with strong "people" skills.

- **Consultant/coach**: Typically outside of an organization, a consultant provides strategic advice, including the development of strategies and solutions. While many consultants have a specialty area, they leverage their abilities in identifying problems, engaging stakeholders, managing projects, and communicating.

What types of roles have you had success in or find intriguing?

Generalist versions of Specialist roles

Another category to consider is the Generalist version of Specialist roles. A small company with a small budget may hire one person who fulfills several needs, choosing adaptive abilities over specialization. Britt Gage, in a series of Substack articles, explores the differences between Specialists and Generalists across various roles and shares an example in marketing.[50]

In this example, a company will hire a marketing Specialist if it is certain of the channel or strategy it intends to pursue. It will need the Specialist's deep knowledge to inform and execute the plan. However, the company might choose a Generalist with marketing experience if it is not entirely sure about its strategy and wants to test and experiment before committing to a direction. A marketing Specialist and a marketing Generalist will differ in how they solve problems, approach work, and impact measures and metrics.

The Specialist will focus on one area, such as email, paid ads, or social media, researching deeply and relying on data to refine that strategy. A marketing Generalist may be more affordable and bring a broader set of skills in areas such as PR, customer experience, and social media. They will also depend on a wide range of experts, cross departments to solve problems, and consider additional metrics when measuring impact. As Gage explains, "While specialists offer deep expertise in specific areas, generalists bring a versatile skill set that enables them to adapt to various challenges and demands."[51]

Entrepreneurial roles

It isn't surprising that many Generalists become entrepreneurs. While being an entrepreneur is not for every Generalist, those who start a business succeed in deploying the best of their talents and then hire Specialists for their expertise. Sohin Shah wrote about the value of the "jack-of-all-trades" in an article for startups.com titled "Being a Generalist is the Foundation of Running Your Own Business."[52] Shah notes that the Generalist's collaboration, creativity, and strong management skills are all essential for dealing with the unexpected nature of a new business.

Many entrepreneurs are Generalists who successfully identify a gap or problem and find ways to solve and address the resulting demand creatively. Entrepreneurs bring a range of abilities, but often share a high degree of risk-taking, a need for speed, and a willingness to experiment, pilot, and test solutions. They are usually attracted to and hire other Generalists in the early stages of organization; people who can similarly range and find ways to build systems quickly, knowing that, with time, those systems will be adjusted.

Jack-of-all-trades

Finally, as Shah points out in her article, it is possible to be and promote oneself as a jack-of-all-trades. However, to do so successfully, we must be clear on the value proposition and tailor the language and example to the audience. A jack-of-all-trades who is clear on their strengths, especially in building trust, learning, and solving problems, is often a good fit for an early-stage company looking for adaptable, all-in team players, or for people to fill an undefined role that needs someone flexible, curious, and willing to try new things.

Job shaping

What about Generalists already in a role they like, but which could be improved upon? Dr. Amy Wrzesniewski of Yale University has researched the impact of job shaping for over twenty years.[53] She defines job shaping as changing the task, relational, and cognitive boundaries of a job. While job shaping does not always apply when safety is a priority (as in the case of air traffic controllers or ship captains), it can occur in many instances and many environments, with or without a manager.

In interviews, Dr. Wrzesniewski shares stories of job shaping that provide concrete examples of what employees do to modify their jobs so they can stay engaged and satisfied, and thrive in their roles. While it is tempting to tailor our job to our interests, it is best to do so in collaboration with the team and manager to ensure that any effort to shape our job does not come at the expense of a colleague or client.

Job shaping can be simple. For example, a schedule change, adding or subtracting tasks, and changing how and with whom one does the work can all change the meaning and boundaries of a job. While some of these changes may seem minor, their impact can be substantial in terms of how employees perceive and perform their roles. Indeed, Wrzesniewski and Adam Grant studied the effect and published a report about job shaping. They found that it ultimately improved retention, upskilling, collective performance, resilience, and relationships.[54]

Job shaping allows us the flexibility to customize jobs to accommodate our strengths as individuals and attributes as Generalists. We might shape an existing role to allow for more autonomy to learn and innovate; pilot and facilitate a solution; assume increased responsibility in one area; or undergo a job rotation in another area. The solutions are numerous, and success, like all role changes, hinges on clearly communicating expectations, responsibilities, salary changes, and accountability.

A Generalist's guide to networking

Networks are vital for any professional moving forward, but they are *essential* for Generalists. In a *Forbes* article describing the different types of networks needed (job searching, peer, and peer transition), the author Jeffrey Ton notes that an estimated seventy percent of jobs are never publicly advertised,[55] making networking even more essential.

Yet the very mention of the word "networking" provokes different reactions. Extroverts may enjoy networking, introverts may find networking awkward and even exhausting, while others may experience networking as transactional at best. As individuals, we might fall into one of these camps, yet as Generalists, networking is essential not just to "get ahead" but because the work we do is dependent on the work of others. This is true whether we are in a job, looking for one, or seeking to learn and connect with a community of like-minded people with similar experiences.

"It's who, not what, you know."

EVERYONE

Moreover, as Generalists, we need a network because it provides us with access to, and support in a market that is built for Specialists. Our network is often the most effective way to find a job, seek a mentor, access resources, or connect with like-minded colleagues and the community. With LinkedIn and other platforms, networking is less insular than before, allowing access to new people and opportunities. Furthermore, as Generalists, we disproportionately benefit from having an active network of advisors and advocates who can speak to our effectiveness in ways that we can't, and that algorithms in search sites prevent us from doing.

Another vital reason for Generalists to network is to avoid the tricky trap of "today, not tomorrow" thinking. As Generalists, we often default to focusing on solving immediate problems of interest and ignore the complicated challenges of a future career. This can be due to the lack of a clear career path, a tendency toward a "spiky career," or having been in one organization and holding multiple roles. Whatever the reason, a robust network can help us think strategically about a career by providing what we can't always get in our current work, including examples of successful Generalist careers, mentors, advisors, new opportunities, learning, and community.

The "give and get" approach

If we approach networking transactionally, we perceive ourselves as perpetual "outsiders" and vulnerable to judgment, rejection, and the fear of not belonging. However, if networking is reframed as *transformational*, the resulting exchanges can lead to authentic connections, opportunities, and growth. Yet, even with this positive, asset-based approach, networking is not easy, which raises the question: How can Generalists network effectively? By bringing our core attributes of curiosity and creative connections to networking (just as we would to any new situation).

There are several "secrets" to networking successfully. The first is that networking is not just about what we "get" but also about what we give: networks thrive because of mutual need and benefit. With this in mind, we can also deliver what we ask for from others. Changing our orientation from giving to taking makes engaging with and sharing with others significantly easier. At its best, networking is symbiotic, and, when embraced, it sparks our curiosity, underscores our interconnectedness, and fosters meaningful connections.

The second secret is that networks need "care and feeding" to remain vital and viable over time. Conveniently, what ensures network vitality is what fuels connections: sharing information, interests, skills, and experiences. A transformational mindset, one that embraces change with curiosity and not fear, allows us to share our networks with others as a way to keep them active and, when needed, serve our purpose. Sharing information is an offering used to connect with others, generate goodwill, and strengthen existing bonds.

The third so-called secret is adopting a learning approach to building a network. Networks do not have to be limited to merely connecting with others. We can collaborate with experts and Specialists who might help us expand our knowledge of an issue, an industry, and more. Having multiple reasons for engaging in networks makes them easier to build, sustain, and, when the time comes, leverage.

Today and tomorrow

Networks can both accelerate and inhibit success, depending on the level of access individuals have. Many employers have eliminated or significantly reduced internal referrals to minimize elevating candidates with privileged connections over those with few, if any. Limiting networks presents something of a conundrum for Generalists. How can we be recommended or draw attention to our candidacy in ways that our CV, screened by AI, cannot?

As Generalists, we need to design our network for our future self, not just for present opportunity. If we can envision the future workplace and the roles we aspire to, we can cultivate a network that reflects what will be, not just what was. Who brings different, interesting points of view? Who might be a future leader? Who shares or needs the kind of strengths you bring? Key areas in which a network is invaluable are grouped for more in-depth exploration: job searching, learning and resources, mentoring and support, and finding a community of like-minded and similarly experienced individuals.

Job searching

Most people rarely connect the grind of a job search with their overall arc of a career. The demands, worry, or ability to discern near-term fit eclipse future planning. Yet, when done right, the job search process can also build the infrastructure to support our long-term careers as Generalists.

Specialists can search for opportunities by title and qualification; an approach that can be challenging and often futile for Generalists. We usually struggle to identify the proper job titles to search for, and even when we find a role of interest, we find it challenging to craft a convincing cover letter or resume that accurately reflects the stated needs and our aligned strengths and skills. And when we do submit a resume and (hopefully) a cover letter, we may fail to pass the unknown AI algorithms serving as gatekeepers and never get to the actual recruiters who review selected applications and determine next steps.

But there is a way forward. By focusing on key factors—ideal environment, core talents, network development, and mentors—and highlighting our individual value proposition, Generalists can find more roles that resonate. We need to consistently reinforce our values while seeking opportunities that enable us to thrive. We must activate our networks by sharing with others what we bring and the opportunities we are seeking, including former colleagues, clients, and managers. While this approach takes longer and demands confidence, it can result not just in a job but in a network that helps us grow and succeed.

Learning and resources

As Generalists, our curiosity can be a calling card when expanding our network. While we need to manage our demands on other people's time, we can learn about others, our work, and, when appropriate, make meaningful connections. A learning mindset positively reframes the business of networking, while a diverse network can be a significant asset at work. Like all learning, the care and curation of knowledge or, in this case, contacts, is essential.

Mentors and advisors

For many, mentors are leaders in their field who can help newer colleagues navigate decisions and challenges in their careers. A newer plumber, doctor, or teacher frequently cites the benefit of a mentor as a resource who can answer hard questions and find the help they need to grow professionally. There is also reverse mentoring, where younger people mentor older colleagues in new technologies, social media, AI, and other areas of expertise brought by younger generations.

Mentoring is popular not only because it is the right thing to do, but also because of its impact on the careers of both the mentor and the mentee. A thirteen-year study (1996–2009) of 1,000 employees involved in a Sun Microsystems mentoring program demonstrated significant benefits. The non-participant retention rate was forty-nine percent. It increased to sixty-nine percent for mentors and seventy-two percent for mentees, saving the company $6.7 million on employee replacement. Both mentors and mentees increased their salary by twenty-eight percent and twenty-five percent respectively, compared with just five percent among non-participants.[56]

Because mentoring is often based on a senior Specialist's expertise and a junior Specialist's interests, it can be a challenge for Generalists to find a mentor who understands their particular strengths, interests, and values. Generalists benefit from mentors who are also Generalists and have experience, advice, and a career they can learn from directly. Generalists who serve as both mentors and mentees also encourage broader awareness and acceptance of the value of Generalists.

There are two types of mentors: career and life mentors. Career mentors serve as coaches or internal advocates, help access gatekeeping opportunities, and make key career decisions. A life mentor can also be important to a Generalist, and provide them with opportunities that are outside their current organization or role. This includes finding people who can help develop, grow, coach, and even manage you as a Generalist (especially when lacking development and growth opportunities in the current work environment).

Mentoring can be both informal and formal. Formal programs are structured around orientation, connections, and development with an eye to promotion for both mentor and mentee. Mentoring is also a meaningful way to support the development and elevation of those who have traditionally been excluded from corporate opportunities, including women and individuals from diverse backgrounds. Informal mentors are essential to an individual's career. Typically, a mentor is identified by a mentee and is supported through advice and introductions, without the need for a formal program.

What strategies can you use to build your network with intention?

Connection and community

While we seek to clarify and communicate our value as Generalists, we do so for ourselves and also for other Generalists. Like the "give and get" approach, there is mutual benefit to publicizing one's abilities as a Generalist as a way to find others. Greater awareness and understanding of Generalists broadly benefits us through increased visibility and value of our capabilities, especially during change. There are many examples of Generalists who have carved a unique path; imagine what they could have done with a broader awareness of Generalists and a community of Generalists. And while each of our paths is necessarily unique, the challenges we face can be better navigated with examples of, and access to other Generalists.

What's next?

Understanding and finding a career direction is critical for Generalists, as is knowing how to develop and grow within their chosen field. Chapter 7 focuses on the areas which Generalists can build upon and grow, including essential competencies for Mature Generalists serving in any capacity.

KEY POINTS

- Generalists who do not plan a career often default to a spiky or squeeze career.

- Several career models align with the attributes of Generalists, including the squiggle, portfolio, and fractional models.

- Generalists need to discern an environment and culture that allows them to:

  - Ask questions, explore possibilities, and actively engage in solving problems;

  - Engage with others, seeking to both understand and receive support from others; and

  - Apply their unique mix of strengths and skills.

- Generalists must discern the right roles and responsibilities that align with their strengths and abilities.

- Job shaping is one way to adapt roles to align with Generalist attributes and organizational needs.

- Generalists deserve managers who understand their value proposition, and can effectively assess performance, and develop key strengths and skills.

- Networking is vital to Generalists, providing avenues and access to opportunities, mentors, learning, community, and more.

QUESTIONS FOR FURTHER REFLECTION

What describes the environments in which you have thrived (and failed) in?

What kind of work inspires you?

How does the Generalist Development Framework in Chapter 3 help direct or support your career path?

WORKBOOK

See section 06 for
additional exercises.

7

GENERALIST
GROWTH

"Education is not the filling
of a pail, but the lighting of a fire."

WILLIAM BUTLER YEATS

THIS BOOK AIMS to both identify and elevate the Generalist, who often feels unseen and unsung, and also provide actionable insights for Generalists navigating a work world built for Specialists.

Wired to learn, the right kinds of professional development help us as Generalists to become better practitioners. However, most of us share the experience of not having our Generalist attributes supported or developed by others. Instead, each of us has figured out how to grow individually, finding ways to build our Generalist attributes even when lacking support to do so. As in previous chapters, we explore how Generalists can continue to guide their growth from Novice to Mature Generalist through three key stages: self-awareness, self-management, and self-development.

Development Arc

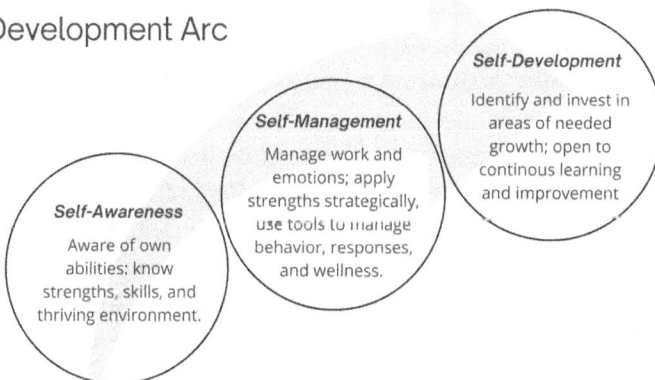

Self-Development

Identify and invest in areas of needed growth; open to continous learning and improvement

Self-Management

Manage work and emotions; apply strengths strategically, use tools to manage behavior, responses, and wellness.

Self-Awareness

Aware of own abilities: know strengths, skills, and thriving environment.

©BigSeaStrategies

An arc of learning and opportunity

Leaving the idea of a traditional career path behind is not the most challenging part of building a career for a Generalist; more difficult is the trap of thinking that knowing our strengths as Generalists constitutes growth. The relief of knowing "what" and who we are, while feeling both wonderful and expansive, is just the beginning of who we can become. Professional development is the intentional growth of who we can be at work. And again, as with our journey thus far, our development as Generalists is one we guide ourselves. As Generalists, we begin by cultivating self-awareness and self-management, the essential scaffolding needed for the self-development we seek.

For Generalists, self-awareness helps us understand that our work is a product of our practice: it is how we each apply our unique strengths, knowledge, and efforts with and for others. Self-awareness enables us to cultivate greater objectivity in our interactions and to seek and integrate feedback more readily. Self-awareness helps us as Generalists be less embarrassed about what we don't know and better at engaging and creating our work "out loud" with others, allowing for curiosity and iteration. Self-awareness necessarily precedes self-management. Many of us have been self-managing parts of our careers and, through trial and error, figured out how to be effective in our roles and collaborate with colleagues. Whereas self-awareness helps us manage ego, self-management encompasses managing our emotions, energy, and work, including setting priorities, organizing work, meeting deadlines, and collaborating with others.

Self-development focuses on our growth as Generalists: What are we learning to improve, excel, and, ultimately, become Mature Generalists? This question is not as easy to answer. Even when we have the confidence and clarity in what we bring, we default to opportunities that do not help us become Mature Generalists. We participate in growth opportunities geared to Specialists because they are available or interesting, but not necessarily what we need to grow as Generalists. Alternatively, we may double down on areas where we already excel and overlook those that could help us better meet the demands of a changing world. We can also get distracted and fail to differentiate between what we need to know now, to attend to current demands, and what we must invest in to meet future needs.

The gap between current and future needs also underscores the case for Generalists to develop if they aspire to be successful leaders intentionally. McKinsey notes that companies in the top quartile for ethnic and cultural diversity (including non-traditional, international, and cross-sector diversity) on executive teams were thirty-three percent more likely to have industry-leading profitability.[57] The Boston Consulting Group confirms that companies with cross-industry leadership are 1.7 times more likely to lead in innovation.[58]

Some of what we learn in self-management easily lends itself to improving in areas of personal growth and development. For example, a system (or systems) that enables us to manage our time more effectively—for example, blocking prime work time, establishing pre-deadlines, or having an accountability partner—will also help us be better managers. We must also skillfully manage our emotions at work in regard to relationships, self-talk, and motivation. Ultimately, we must cultivate our essential skills ("soft skills") to navigate the stress and change that define a complicated and changing world. Together, self-awareness, self-management, and self-development combine to create an arc of learning and opportunity that we, as Generalists, can name and navigate.

As we become better at being a Generalist, we can also be more intentional about how we grow and develop skills that bring additional value to our capacity as Mature Generalists. Some skills help refine our core attributes, making us better practitioners and partners. These are often the skills that effective leaders need, which is not surprising given that forty percent of people in the C-suite are Generalists. These key skills include listening, general management, decision-making, giving and receiving feedback, and utilizing feedback effectively. We'll explore each of these in the sections that follow.

What practices and approaches have helped you become more self-aware?

Learning to listen, listening to learn

As Generalists, we are often open to changing our minds; "why" and "what if" seem to run on a constant loop in our brains. And yet this relentless and ranging curiosity can block what we need to manage and develop our curiosity—our ability to listen.

"We have two ears and
one mouth, so we can listen
twice as much as we speak."

EPICTETUS

Listening, not asking, is the cornerstone of curiosity. How we hear is the difference between a Generalist who loves to learn and one who understands what is said. For those of us who aspire to manage others or lead, listening is arguably the most important and necessary skill. Our ability as Generalists to effectively curate what we learn requires what deep listening offers—a way to discern what is essential *and* seek understanding. Listening, as Oscar Trimboli defines it in his book *How to Listen*, is not a matter of just slowing down, and adopting a calm facial expression and a neutral body posture. Nor is it a matter of only training your ears. It is a multi-sensory practice, essential to seeking understanding, leading, and meeting the demands of our rapidly changing world.

Most of us do a great job of listening. Trimboli shares that most people believe they are *six times* better at listening than others.[59] But the data tells a different story: speaking happens at 125 words a minute, listening at 400 words a minute, and the average thinking speed is an astonishing 900 words a minute. These different speeds cause gaps between talking and thinking that result in confusion, misunderstandings, assumptions, and misinterpretations. We confuse our listening and thinking based on the speed at which we do both, making the mistake that our ability to think quickly is a result of our ability to listen deeply. A familiar trap for everyone, it is a perilous trap for senior leaders, who must listen with greater attention than others because the hierarchy of power often discourages speaking openly.

Being a good listener is not just the difference between what is said, heard, and then thought about; listening is a profound practice that requires awareness and deep focus. Trimboli describes listening as a "contact sport" and, like all sports, practice determines performance. Trimboli's five levels of listening—how we prepare, what we hear, the backstory, what is unsaid, and meaning—offer a ladder of learning and practice that transforms how we think about and approach listening. Generalists who become better listeners show up differently and with discernment to the learnings we constantly seek.

In his book, Trimboli guides readers and listeners alike through a learning process to explore what is said and, more importantly, what is *unsaid*—unspoken meanings and unverbalized problems. Expanding beyond the ear's rewards, listeners are treated to a deeper understanding, fewer misunderstandings, and healthier, more trusting relationships. And, perhaps most importantly for the Generalist, they are rewarded with more "opportunities to think, hear, and see complex challenges differently."

Effective listening begins with individual preparation. Eliminating distractions and ego allows us to give and pay attention while listening. Typically, we listen with a tendency to detect similarities—what we share with the listener—or differences. Yet when we learn how to listen to what is being said with an emphasis on how—the emphases, biases, and attention gaps, to name a few—we can ensure the conversation will result in more than what is agreed or disagreed. Listening requires all of our senses, allowing us to gather much more information than hearing alone can provide.

While a word can be spoken, the timing and energy behind it may change its meaning; consider the word "right" and how it can translate to "yes," "wrong," "agree," a question, sarcasm, and so much more based on tone alone. Bringing our whole selves to listening is essential both in the moment and in seeking to understand the backstory of how this moment came to be. While some may think it's a waste of time, requesting and listening to their backstory gives the speaker a chance to establish context, diminish assumptions, and be heard. It also helps both near-term and long-term problem-solving.

When we listen to what is being said, and how it's being said, it is often the unsaid where meaning emerges. If two people conversing have a misunderstanding, imagine how many more misunderstandings happen in a group conversation with variations in the ability to listen deeply. It is in moments like these that listening skills can differentiate the maturity and capability of both managers and leaders.

Being intentional in developing listening skills and finding ways to practice each step benefits Generalists across all core attributes—

curiosity, creative connection-making, and context—enhancing our ability to learn more rapidly and solve problems more readily.

Oscar's book, podcasts, and other resources provide step-by-step instructions to a transformative understanding of how we seek and assimilate information. We can be light, easy, and straightforward when present and listening to others.

LISTEN LIKE A LEADER

- To encourage more effective listening in virtual or in-person meetings, commit to silencing phones and minimizing distractions. Ensure screens are on, and, when needed, explain why.
- Keep an open mind, rather than listening for agreement or disagreement.
- Actively practice listening with others.
- Assess increased listening abilities as demonstrated by more effective meetings, fewer misunderstandings, etc.
- Ask senior leaders how they learned to listen, including when they wish they had heard more deeply.
- Explore the difference between intuiting solutions and listening for solutions.

Curiosity and curation

Often, our love of learning something new is itself a satisfying experience. Yet as Generalists, our "ranging" curiosity presents an ongoing challenge of managing what we know. The more we ask, the more we know, and the greater the demand for our ability to use what we learn astutely and appropriately.

As Generalists, we might find our curiosity broad and distracting in our early career. We ask questions, dive down rabbit holes, and chase one interesting idea after another, regardless of current need or potential value. For curiosity to be effective for Generalists, it must lead to usable information and insights. Like a tailor making a suit, we need more material than we end up using, yet, like an adventurer without a destination, we do not know precisely what we will need for the journey.

Our need for more information is driven by our desire to learn, but its effectiveness lies in how to manage our curiosity. A Mature Generalist knows when we have learned enough and avoids distractions while still scanning for new information. A Mature Generalist also understands how to curate and deploy learning, knowing when to dig deeper and provide the right-sized support to the problem or need.

THINK LIKE A CURATOR

- Essential or interesting? We may not always know which questions are necessary or which questions are valuable. Still, we can improve our ability to discern by prioritizing questions as essential and secondary to what we are seeking to understand. Try AI to do the following:

  - Find and filter quality content and information, including questions.

  - Organize information by using AI to tag content based on issues, categories, and other relevant criteria.

  - Create your learning sequence by using AI to assess your knowledge (based on past queries and input) and recommend information on what you need to learn next.

  - Summarize one or more longer resources (such as videos), including identifying complex issues.

  - Search by concept or relationship using an advanced AI engine.

  - Manage and refresh learning by using AI to track your progress and remind you when to review.

  - Identify patterns across information using AI to find how ideas from one field are used in another.

- Use knowledge management. A system to access and share learning can be beneficial to Generalists. Some suggestions include:

  - Organize your inbox or use a folder to save and sort items for weekly review and relevant sharing.

  - Actively contribute as a user of your organization's knowledge management system.

  - Share a relevant learning experience or insight at a team meeting, or host a "brown bag" or "grand round" on a topic of interest.

  - Create or join a community of practice and meet regularly on a shared topic, purpose, or issue.

  - Create a Slack channel or a team wiki for tracking, sharing, and building key trends or big-picture issues relevant to your work.

  - Create new project-based teams to diminish silos and increase shared knowledge and collaboration.

  - Integrating sharing and development into existing work, such as mid-project process reviews or post-engagement debriefs.

  - Capture new ideas regularly through sessions, an "idea hopper," or other means.

- Set aside time to learn for learning's sake. Allow for limited "tunneling" into a topic of interest.

What areas of development do you think you should invest in?

Discernment and decisions

The ability to discern options and make informed decisions is essential for managers and leaders alike. Given competing demands and limited resources, decision-making is rarely easy and always entails a cost of what is not done. It is even more challenging during times of change when decisions must be made quickly, without complete information, and potentially have an enormous impact on the work and livelihood of employees. As Generalists seeking leadership positions, we must learn to look to the future with equanimity, discern trends, and seek diverse opinions to make decisions. This involves risk and being wrong, depending on the vagaries of time.

To practice a better way to make decisions as Generalists, we must first understand conventional decision-making, which typically aligns with linear thinking and details a step-by-step process with a logical conclusion:

1   Identify the problem
2   Gather relevant information
3   Identify options
4   Assess your options
5   Make a choice
6   Implement the decision
7   Evaluate the outcome

A linear and logical process is effective for decisions where choices must be rationally ruled out or selected. However, linear decision-making is less effective during ambiguous times when little information or time is available. As Generalists, we can leverage our core attributes during times of change by knowing the amount of information we need (cue curiosity and curation) and discerning one or more possible directions based on the desired outcome (cue creative connections and context).

The challenge is not how we make decisions, but that we assume our process, so apparent to us, is often invisible to others. Making our thinking process explicit helps. Compare the linear approach with the approach to decision-making that a Mature Generalist takes:

1 Identify (evaluate) the desired outcome of the current challenge
2 Identify (intuit) possible options
3 Solicit Specialist input on options
4 Make and communicate a choice
5 Implement, test, and evaluate
6 Iterate as needed

Communicating our decision-making process is essential for Generalists seeking leadership. However, effective decision-making goes further, and Mature Generalists will recognize that changes in information and context can impact decisions. Change affects not only how we make decisions, but also how we continue to improve and iterate our decision-making. To become better at making iterative decisions, we must ask and continue to refine our answers to these essential questions:

- How do we learn to make decisions that have real consequences?
- How do we manage risk and responsibility?
- How do we decide with insufficient information?
- How do we communicate decisions?

Decision-making can be complex, even when the decision itself seems unimportant (e.g., menu options at a restaurant). To become more confident in making more complex decisions, we must start small and practice making decisions that do not have significant consequences. Reinterpreting decisions already made using Generalist insights can be another way to practice (and play with) decision-making.

DISCERN AND DECIDE

- **Manage up**—As Generalists, we can help discern information, curate key questions and ideas, ask Specialists for input on a process, and even suggest language to communicate effectively.

- **Seek Advice**—Find mentors who have faced similar decisions. They will understand the process and engage in a deeper conversation about how and why a decision was made.

- **Adopt a learner's mindset**—Interrogate past decisions to understand differing information and scenarios better.

- **Pressure-test**—Generalists can pressure-test each stage of the decision-making process with additional questions, including:

  - What is the ideal outcome?

  - How does that outcome evolve in a changing environment?

  - What information do we need and have access to?

  - What information is ideal but unknown?

  - What information do stakeholders, including Specialists, need to share and know?

  - What do people need to know to accept the decision?

  - What are the best ways to communicate the decision?

What is your current decision-making process, and how can it be improved?

Giving and receiving feedback

While feedback is essential to growth, the word itself can elicit a range of responses from welcome and actionable to unhelpful and rejection, based on how people experience feedback. Ideally, feedback is given based on the responsibilities detailed in a job description and in an actionable way. Yet, a job description rarely names the capabilities that Generalists seek to improve for their growth (curiosity, creative connections, and context). All too often, this approach results in Generalists receiving input based on Specialist competencies, not their own, or suggestions that are neither relevant nor actionable.

To get what they need, Generalists can choose to initiate feedback on their priorities for improvement in addition to any feedback needed to perform their current role. Check-ins and performance reviews are good times to solicit more relevant and actionable input that further develops core Generalist attributes and individual strengths:

- **Curiosity**—We seek to understand how we use our curiosity as a finely tuned instrument, balancing knowing too little or asking too much. Feedback on curiosity should relate to the quality of questions, research, and curation. Ask for examples, as well as support for asking better questions and curating information.

- **Creative connections**—At its best, our "out-of-the-box" thinking and solution-seeking balances ideation and discernment. Feedback on making connections should focus on the quality of your solutions and your ability to engage and manage those involved.

- **Context**—Discernment demands ongoing development, as does the ability to function in differing environments. Feedback on navigating the operational environment should help identify and support what you need to thrive (freedom, culture, etc.).

- **Communication**—Being an effective communicator is an area of growth for everyone. Still, for Generalists who do not have the shorthand of Specialist credentials, titles, and more, effective communication is crucial. Generalists should seek specific feedback on the efficacy of their value proposition, solutions, and relationship management.

- **Individual Strengths**—Generalists who understand their strengths can seek feedback on how they are using them to support or distract from success.

When leading, Mature Generalists often manage processes, projects, and people, so knowing how to give actionable and welcome feedback is essential. Yet giving effective feedback can be difficult. Misaligned performance metrics, personal differences, poor management, and ineffective communication can cloud input received at work. A Gallup study on employee performance found that "only 14% of employees strongly agree their performance reviews inspire them to improve. In other words, if performance reviews were a drug, they would not meet the FDA approval for efficacy."[60]

And even when we learn from our mistakes, we do not always know how to transform that feeling of failure and shame into learning and opportunity. This can be a particular problem in performance reviews, where failure may be both a strike against overall performance and a source of shame, eliminating the opportunity for effective feedback to develop and grow.

"The greatest
teacher is failure."

YODA

Most feedback is determined by who is delivering the feedback and its content—positive, negative, performance, 360 reviews, peer insights, and so on—and not by the person receiving the feedback. Too often, we default to a frank approach to feedback from the perspective of the "giver," rather than one that's relevant and actionable by the "receiver." Those who give feedback are far more successful in getting the desired behavior when they focus on how the receiver prefers to get feedback. This makes it easier to tailor input that is accepted and acted upon.

In addition to centering the recipient, those seeking to give practical feedback need to understand that the "even split" between positive and constructive feedback is a fallacy: one positive piece of feedback is not "balanced" by a constructive (negative) piece of feedback. According to a study completed by Marcial Losada and Emily Heaphy in 2004, high-performing teams have five positive comments for every single critical comment.[61] Other experts suggest that criticism should be proportionate to performance. For example, when ninety percent of the performance is positive, the same ratio should apply to feedback.

There needs to be enough information, but not too much, to facilitate active reflection and meaningful discussion. Starting with positive reflections reinforces what works, builds good intentions, strengthens trust, and provides the recipient with a context in which to metabolize challenging feedback. An individualized approach will increase receptivity and lay a foundation for future growth. How someone likes to receive feedback is foundational and should be part of onboarding or manager training.

A FIVE-POINT FEEDBACK CHECKLIST

1 **Know the recipient's strengths**—Understanding others' strengths provides the person giving feedback with insights into how the recipient can best receive and apply feedback. Effective feedback is defined by the recipient's ability to metabolize and take action, not the giver's precision or eloquence.

2 **Be specific**—Feedback is not the time for airing grievances. Feedback should focus on a particular situation or action, rather than encompassing what a person may or may not have done.

3 **Start positive**—Share what worked—all of it—and then what didn't work, but just part of it. For more constructive feedback, it is essential to prioritize what to share, allow the recipient to reflect, and incorporate their thoughts while being mindful not to dwell too much on what went wrong. Focusing solely on what didn't work can undermine the effectiveness of positive feedback.

4 **Provide actionable feedback**—Name the desired change. Clearly outline what to retain and repeat, as well as what to modify. Only addressing the latter will rob the recipient of insight into how to replicate success. While positive feedback is essential, it is equally important that it is specific and names exactly what worked in a way that the person receiving the feedback understands, appreciates, and can replicate.

5 **Map a simple path forward**—Agree on the next step, but just one. Learning from failure demands a level of curiosity and discomfort rather than learning from success. So, while feedback may suggest multiple improvements, choosing just one to address will more likely result in improvement and allow for the next step to be determined and implemented.

What does a successful learning and growth path look like to you?

Developing community

While improving one's abilities and creating a rewarding career as a Generalist is possible, a greater challenge is finding a community of other Generalists. We are invisible to everyone, including each other. Yet, it is both affirming and energizing when we see someone else with whom we have the shared experience of living and working "outside" of accepted careers: we are not alone! By publicly embracing our value as Generalists, we both signal to and invite others to do the same, elevating our collective value. Community is also how we can help each other grow, improve, and better meet the challenges we face. Participation and collaboration with Specialists will always be central to our success. Being part of a community—online, in person—with other Generalists helps everyone meet the increasing demands and needs of rapid change.

What does community mean to you?

KEY POINTS

- Generalists must be self-aware and have rudimentary self-management to engage in effective self-development.

- Self-awareness is essential for self-management, and strengths can serve as valuable tools in maintaining positive habits. This encompasses managing tasks related to work, emotions, and relationships.

- Developing key skills helps Generalists become better experts and likely leaders. These include listening, curation, and decision-making.

- A community of Generalists helps us reinforce our values.

QUESTIONS FOR FURTHER REFLECTION

What other areas of development do you think would be helpful to you?

How can you use the Generalist Development Framework to better understand your current status as a Generalist and the areas in which you need to grow and develop?

What unique impact will you bring as a Mature Generalist?

WORKBOOK

See section 07 for
additional exercises.

"The mysteries of the trade
become no mysteries
but are, as it were, in the air."

ALFRED MARSHALL

CONCLUSION
THE OVERSTORY

N CHAPTER 1, we were introduced to the catalytic conversations of David Epstein and Malcolm Gladwell, in which they shed light on how to be excellent and expert, both of which are essential to success and performance. And yet neither Epstein nor Gladwell ventured to explain how Generalists differ in their definition of both. Epstein provided many examples of successful Generalists (Federer, van Gogh, and Frances Hesselbein, to name a few) in making his case for *why* Generalists thrive in a Specialist world, and encouraged the exploration of Generalist qualities more broadly. However, he did not explain how Generalists can *be* in a Specialist world. Interestingly, a metaphor from Gladwell's new book does.

In the fall of 2024, Malcolm Gladwell published *Revenge of the Tipping Point*, twenty-five years after his bestseller, *The Tipping Point*, explored the essential criteria for incubating and creating change. Gladwell's 1999 book featured palatable examples borrowed mainly from the corporate world. His new book tackles grittier, more realistic, and more complex challenges, including global epidemics (COVID-19), affirmative action, suicide, crime, and other "wicked" problems we face today.

In late 2024, writing on Substack, David Epstein shared a conversation he had with Gladwell about *Revenge of the Tipping Point*. Epstein remarked how much he liked the metaphor of the "overstory" to explain how communities differ in response to change. The overstory refers to the upper canopy of trees; its composition and chemistry influence the understory (shorter, shade-tolerant trees) and the surrounding vegetation (assorted shrubs, bushes, and undergrowth). The ecosystem of the upper tree canopy differs from the rest of the tree, and is focused on communicating with other trees via chemical signals to prevent tree tops from crowding and blocking the stream of light to the forest floor. Like the fungi network that connects the root systems underground, the overstory is unseen but vital to the entire ecosystem.

As Epstein explained, an overstory is "around everything, but you're not paying attention to it in an explicit manner." He said it reminded him of the nineteenth-century English economist Alfred Marshall, who "was talking about cities, and when people live nearby, he said: 'The mysteries of the trade become no mysteries but are, as it were, in the air.' He's talking about how people learn trades and skills without being formally trained."[62] In this quote, if we substitute "the trade" for "Generalists," we can see how the overstory becomes an apt metaphor: "The mysteries of Generalists become no mysteries. Still, they are, as it were, in the air."

As Generalists, much of what we do can seem invisible—and yet we are everywhere and without mystery. Like the overstory, Generalists are engaged in a constant and dynamic dialogue with change: information exists, is responded to, iterated upon, metabolized, exists again, and the evolution continues. Indeed, our curiosity, creativity, and adaptive approach to problems are "as it were, in the air."

The metaphor of the overstory explains how we have evolved as inextricable to context and collaboration and how essential we are to navigating change. Our purpose as Generalists is to make the "overstory" we engage with explicit, accessible, and actionable. In essence, we want to be seen and recognized in the ways Specialists already are. Not to feed the ego or pride, but because we make change visible. Like the crowns of the trees that reach for the light, we must continuously adjust and adapt to the larger context in which we thrive and help others to do the same. We cannot be satisfied—nor do others expect or want us to be—with a default to the status quo, with definitions that obscure or diminish our purpose in mapping the unknown.

The makings of Mature Generalists

As Generalists, we can no longer let ourselves be defined by others, hide behind the enthusiasm of the Novice, the endless curiosity of the Distracted, or the "fake it 'til you make it" persistence of the Dissatisfied. We can't blame others for being unseen and unsung, or even ourselves for doubting our value. And we can't ignore the powerful strengths we each bring and that are needed to tackle the challenges we face. The Generalist Development Framework helps us meet the moment by helping us better understand ourselves, be seen by others, and create a career we love. We have what we need to succeed: a definition, our strengths, a framework, and a growing demand for our unique abilities at a time when they are much needed.

As we endeavor to be Mature Generalists, we are seeking to become the best of what a practitioner is—an expert at adaptation. Like the master gardeners who continuously evolve their gardens, finding the right spot for each plant or the calibration of the tree canopy, we can use the changing context to create the kinds of environments in which we can all meaningfully thrive. Who we each become as Mature Generalists matters to us, of course, but even more to others.

A MATURE GENERALIST

- Is committed to best practices for practitioners, including a learning mindset
- Is skillfully adaptive
- Knows where and how they function best
- Has a nuanced understanding and keen control of their curiosity
- Curates and applies knowledge judiciously
- Identifies and seeks to solve problems quickly and inclusively
- Will play with ideas and test solutions
- Takes considered risks and understands failure as a learning

- Moves from role to role with intention and learning
- Understands the capacity of self and others
- Has strong "people" skills
- Often leads or manages teams, projects, or organizations
- Utilizes strong decision-making skills, even with missing information
- Knows what they need to succeed
- Depends on and supports Specialists
- Quickly spots talent and mentors Generalists
- Aligns their practice with purpose, and purpose with values

As we pursue excellence in practice, we do so with purpose, aligned with what matters to us and the change we seek to influence. Our values, both individual and shared, help us when nothing else can. Values help us make the right decisions when information is lacking; values help us prioritize when we're faced with too many choices; values help us understand that striving for impact is better than seeking perfection. Values are, like all of a Mature Generalist's work, an intentional practice.

There's a saying that "we go faster alone and further together." The changes required of the future demand the latter. Being in community with other Generalists allows us to quickly access our confidence, communicate our value, and create successful careers. We succeed when we accept that, individually and together as Generalists, we thrive in ambiguity by asking questions, identifying needs, and spotting connections to ensure alignment. We begin to find a clear way forward when we have the benefit of doing it with others.

Our collective overstory provides us with a sense of community and reassurance that we are not alone as we strive to meet the demands of a changing world. Yet, as we navigate the complex, chaotic, and rapidly evolving future, we must continually ask ourselves how we can genuinely embrace and activate our Generalist value.

Parting words

If we are to remember anything as Generalists, it is this:

- **Practice**—In a world full of Specialists, as Generalists, we are not experts in specific areas of information, but instead experts in practice: of learning, trying, revising, improving, and making decisions in ambiguous moments and fast-changing circumstances.

- **Pilot**—In the spirit of learning, we like to test new ideas, innovate improvements, and figure out what works and, importantly, what doesn't.

- **Partnerships**—As Generalists, we need others both as the source of our learning and the evidence of our success. We need the expertise of Specialists from whom to learn, as well as the problems that emerge in between.

- **People, Process, Product**—We are often in a position to manage because we function in the "in-between," seeking information and providing solutions.

- **Power**—Adaptability and variability are a source of power for Generalists: change is our medium—it demands what we do best. That is, using our curiosity and lateral thinking to adapt, and giving us what we need most: variability.

A book can require a significant amount of space to explain an idea, incorporating research, case studies, and examples to support it. But in the end, the concept can be summed up far more succinctly. For this book, the idea is this: *As a Generalist, you can find the confidence you seek, communicate your value effectively, and ultimately carve a career you love.*

With that said, here are my parting words to you:

- Generalists are essential and needed now more than ever.

- There is no widely accepted definition of Generalist—we can change that!

- There is not just one path. There is only your path, and it may look very different from others'.

- Strengths are to Generalists as skills are to Specialists.

- The better you define and communicate your value proposition, the better positioned you are for a role.

- Generalists have key priorities to establish in their career framework.

- Networks are essential.

- Your impact contributes to your reputation.

- Your values will guide you.

- The time for Generalists is now.

ACKNOWLEDGMENTS

NOTHING WORTHWHILE IS done alone; I have many people to thank for their support and contributions, known and unknown, to this book and my work more broadly. As mentioned in the introduction, I never would have started writing this book if not for the many conversations with and encouragement of Andrea McGrath. Andrea passed away unexpectedly in October 2024, and the many memories people have since shared of her spirited generosity, keen intelligence, and unrelenting commitment to making the world a better and brighter place are a testament to the mark she made. This book is dedicated to both her memory and example.

The Expert Author Community provided me with a platform to learn, build, write, and publish a book. My book is a reflection of what a community can do: from the direction of Kelly Irving's curriculum and coaching, to the larger community's support and feedback, to the nitty-gritty of accountability, this book is as much a result of the support of many others as it is of my persistence. Special thanks to EAC members Monique Zytnik, Jennifer Doyle Vancil, TyAnn Osborn, Chloe Temple, Salli Cohen, and EAC members Paul Watkins, Taural Rhoden, Lea Rausch, Penelope Barr, and Oscar Trimboli, for their generous insights and support. A special shout-out to coach community convener Charlotte Blair, whose writing journey inspired mine, the introduction to Janine Garner, and to the many coaches of the Connect, Learn Share community who teach me something new every day.

The great writing teacher Natalie Goldberg understands writing as a practice to study the mind; I have found long-form writing to be exactly that and so much more. The opportunity to engage with ideas on the page was an exhilarating and yet never lonely process. I am grateful to the many who shared their own experiences as Generalists in a changing world. They include: Michelle Auger, Ashley Powers, Nate Wong, Jessica Brooks, Katie Potter, Carissa Holsted, Jessica Bearman, Gabriel Rhoads, Michelle Powers, Jay Vilar, Tanja Schroeder, Steve Fleckenstein, Susan Skrupa among many others. Thanks to Erin Cox for partnering in piloting my Generalist course, and the many friends and family who sparked ideas and knowingly supported my efforts. Just as Andrea catalyzed my journey, Tina Cassidy ensured I finished, serving as my first reader, editor, cheerleader, and all-around book mentor. Thank you, Tina!

Most importantly, I would like to extend a special thank you to the many individual and organizational clients and colleagues who have helped me grow not only as a coach, but also in my confidence and capabilities in raising the visibility and value of other Generalists.

I see you!

SUGGESTED READING

Range: Why Generalists Triumph in a Specialized World by David Epstein

The Neo-Generalist by Kenneth Mikkelsen and Richard Martin

Emotional Agility: Get Unstuck, Embrace Change, and Thrive in Work and Life by Susan David, PhD

The Squiggly Career: Ditch the Ladder, Discover Opportunity, Design Your Career by Helen Tupper and Sarah Ellis

Find Your Why: A Practical Guide for Discovering Purpose for You and Your Team by Simon Sinek

Career Unstuck: How to Play to Your Strengths to Find Freedom and Purpose in Your Work Again by Charlotte Blair

How to Listen: Discover the Hidden Key to Better Communication by Oscar Trimboli

Pivot: The Only Move That Matters is Your Next One by Jenny Blake

Thinking Fast and Slow by Daniel Kahneman

It's Who You Know: How a Network of 12 Key People Can Fast-Track Your Success by Janine Garner

O.C. Tanner's 2023 *Global Culture Report*

The Case for a Generalist: The Non-Profits MVP by Sue Dahling Sullivan for BridgeSpan

NOTES

1   Or: jack-of-all-trades, multi-hyphenate, utility player, "a doer," Renaissance thinker, unicorn, hobbyist, dabbler, etc.

2   Siobhán O'Riordan, "The Generalist's Dilemma," *LinkedIn*, December 5, 2024, https://www.linkedin.com/posts/saoriordan_i-first-published-this-article-in-july-2022-activity-7270522192109436931-2WAr.

3   David Epstein, *Range: Why Generalists Triumph in a Specialized World* (New York: Riverhead Books, 2019), 107.

4   "Rise of the Generalist," O.C. Tanner *Culture Report Home*, accessed March 7, 2025, https://www.octanner.com/global-culture-report/2023-rise-of-the-generalist.

5   Elena Lytkina Botelho, Kim Rosenkoetter Powell, and Nicole Wong, "The Fastest Path to the CEO Job, According to a 10-Year Study," *Harvard Business Review*, January 31, 2018, https://hbr.org/2018/01/the-fastest-path-to-the-ceo-job-according-to-a-10-year-study.

6   "The 2020s Will Be a Decade of Upskilling. Employers Should Take Notice," *World Economic Forum Annual Meeting*, January 2024, accessed April 6, 2025, https://www.weforum.org/stories/2024/01/the-2020s-will-be-a-decade-of-upskilling-employers-should-take-notice/.

7   Isaiah Berlin, *The Hedgehog and the Fox* (United Kingdom: Weidenfeld & Nicolson, 1953), www.blogs.hss.ed.ac.uk/crag/files/2016/06/the_hedgehog_and_the_fox-berlin.pdf.

8   Robert Greene, *Greene's Groats-Worth of Wit*, (Pamphlet, 1592), https://www.google.com/books/edition/Greene_s_Groats_worth_of_Wit/o2VIAQAAMAAJ?hl=en&gbpv=1&pg=PA8&printsec=frontcover.

9   Howard R. Gold, "How the Steam Engine Spurred Modern Cities," *Chicago Booth Review—Economics*, December 3, 2018, https://www.chicagobooth.edu/review/how-steam-engine-spurred-modern-cities.

10 Dennis Abrams, *The Inventions of the Moving Assembly Line: A Revolution in Manufacturing* (New York: Chelsea House, 2011), 68.

11   Peter Cappelli, "The End of GE's Crotonville: What It Says About L&D," *HRExecutive.com*, November 15, 2022, www.hrexecutive.com/the-end-of-ges-crotonville-what-it-says-about-ld.

12   Peter Drucker, *The Effective Executive* (New York: Harper & Row, 1967), 101.

13   Jim Collins, *Good to Great* (New York: Harper Business, 2001).

14   Kenneth Mikkelsen and Richard Martin, *The Neo-Generalist* (London: LID Publishing Ltd., 2016), 34.

15   It's worth noting that Generalists in human resources and social work alone have an acknowledged Generalist role, including a title. An HR Generalist typically performs almost all necessary responsibilities. A Generalist social worker is similarly deployed based on client needs and demands.

16   "What are Industry 4.0, the Fourth Industrial Revolution, and 4IR?" *McKinsey*, August 17, 2022, www.mckinsey.com/featured-insights/mckinsey-explainers/what-are-industry-4-0-the-fourth-industrial-revolution-and-4ir.

17   Warren Bennis and Burt Nanus, *Leaders: The Strategies for Taking Charge* (New York: Harper & Row, 1985).

18   Andy Kemp, "Employee Wellbeing Hinges on Management, Not Work Mode," *Gallup Blog*, August 15, 2024, www.gallup.com/workplace/648500/employee-wellbeing-hinges-management-not-work-mode.aspx.

19   Te-Ping Chen, "Remote Workers Are Losing Out on Promotions, New Data Shows," *WSJ.com*, January 11, 2024, www.wsj.com/lifestyle/careers/remote-workers-are-losing-out-on-promotions-8219ec63.

20   "What is Wellbeing and Why Does it Matter?" *Gallup Services*, accessed June 22, 2025, www.gallup.com/workplace/404105/importance-of-employee-wellbeing.aspx.aspx.

21   Ellyn Maese, "Almost a Quarter of the World Feels Lonely," *Gallup Blog*, October 24, 2023, www.news.gallup.com/opinion/gallup/512618/almost-quarter-world-feels-lonely.aspx.

22   O.C. Tanner, *Rise of the Generalist.*

23   Tim Harford, *The Data Detective: Ten Easy Rules to Make Sense of Statistics* (New York: Riverhead Books, 2021).

24   Dan Kahan, "Five Dimensions of Curiosity," *Medium*, January 4, 2018. www.toddkashdan.medium.com/what-are-the-five-dimensions-of-curiosity-7de73684d53a.

25   George Loewenstein, "The Psychology of Curiosity: A Review and Reinterpretation," *Psychological Bulletin* 116, no. 1 (July 1994): 75–98, www.researchgate.net/publication/232440476_The_Psychology_of_Curiosity_A_Review_and_Reinterpretation.

26   Mario Livio, "The Why Behind Asking Why: The Science of Curiosity," *Knowledge at Wharton Podcast*, August 2017, 1 min., 23 sec., www.knowledge.wharton.upenn.edu/podcast/knowledge-at-wharton-podcast/makes-us-curious.

27 Edward de Bono, *The Use of Lateral Thinking* (London: Jonathan Cape, 1967).

28 Daniel Kahneman, *Thinking, Fast and Slow* (New York: Farrar, Straus and Giroux, 2011).

29 Peter Senge, *The Fifth Discipline: The Art & Practice of the Learning Organization* (New York: Doubleday, 1994).

30 Diane Hamilton, "Curiosity Code Index," accessed March 17, 2024, www .drdianehamilton.com/curiosity-code-system/curiosity-code-index/.

31 "The History of CliftonStrengths," *Gallup*, accessed September 22, 2024, www.gallup.com/cliftonstrengths/en/253754/history-cliftonstrengths.aspx.

32 Adam Grant, "Here's the Four-Step Plan to Finding Your Strengths—and Your Life's Calling," *Quartz*, originally appeared on LinkedIn, updated July 21, 2022, www.qz.com/100120/heres-the-four-step-plan-to-find-your-strengths-and-maybe-your-lifes-calling.

33 Rob Desimone, "Improve Work Performance with a Focus on Employee Development," *Gallup.com*, December 12, 2019, www.gallup.com/workplace/ 269405/high-performance-workplaces-differently.aspx.

34 Jonathan Swift, "The Battle of the Books," in Miscellanies (London: Published posthumously, 1704).

35 Jim Harter, "U.S. Employee Engagement Sinks to 10-Year Low," *Gallup.com*, January 14, 2025, www.gallup.com/workplace/654911/employee-engage-ment-sinks-year-low.aspx.

36 Ashley Reichheld and Amelia Dunlop, *The Four Factors of Trust* (Hoboken, NJ: Wiley, 2022), www.deloitte.com/us/en/about/four-factors-of-trust.html.

37 Marija Kojic, "Workplace Communication Statistics in 2025," *Pumble*, updated February 11, 2025, www.pumble.com/learn/communication/ communication-statistics/.

38 Andrea Alexander, Aaron De Smet, Meredith Langstaff, and Dan Ravid, "McKinsey Report on the Future of Work," *McKinsey & Company*, April 1, 2001, www.mckinsey.com/capabilities/people-and-organizational-performance/ our-insights/what-employees-are-saying-about-the-future-of-remote-work.

39 Daniel D. Dressler, MD, MSC, MHM, FACP, "Hospitalist Growth in the U.S.," *Jwatch.com*, February 16, 2023, www.jwatch.org/na55794/2023/02/16/ hospitalist-growth-us.

40 O.C. Tanner, *Rise of the Generalist*.

41 John Adair, *100 Greatest Ideas for Effective Leadership* (Oxford: Capstone, 2002).

42 O.C. Tanner, *Rise of the Generalist*.

43 Allie Kelly, "Half of Gen Z Workers Think ChatGPT Gives Better Career Advice Than Their Manager, Survey Says of Gen Z," *Business Insider*, February 13, 2024, www.businessinsider.com/gen-z-ai-chatgpt-for-career-advice-motivation-workplace-2024-2.

44 Robert N. Llewellyn, "The Four Career Concepts," *SHRM.org*, September 1, 2002, www.shrm.org/topics-tools/news/hr-magazine/four-career-concepts.

45 Helen Tupper and Sarah Ellis, *The Squiggly Career* (London: Penguin, 2020).

46 Christina Wallace, *The Portfolio* (New York: Balance, 2023).

47 "5 Reasons for the Rise in Fractional Executive Jobs in 2024," *MDLPartners. com*, www.mdl-partners.com/5-reasons-for-the-rise-in-fractional-cxo-work/.

48 Ryan Pendell, "5 Ways Managers Can Stop Employee Turnover," *Gallup. com*, published November 10, 2021, www.gallup.com/workplace/357104/ ways-managers-stop-employee-turnover.aspx.

49 Elena Lytkina Botelho, Kim Rosenkoetter Powell, and Nicole Wong, "The Fastest Path to the CEO Job, According to a 10-Year Study," *Harvard Business Review*, February 1, 2018, www.hbr.org/2018/01/the-fastest-path-to-the-ceo-job-according-to-a-10-year-study.

50 Britt Gage, "How Generalists Help Generalist Founders," *How We Do (Substack)*, August 15, 2024, www.ofalltrades.substack.com/p/how-generalists-help-generalist-founders.

51 Ibid.

52 Sohin Shah, "Being a Generalist is the Foundation of Running Your Own Business," *Startups.com*, www.startups.com/library/expert-advice/ generalist-business.

53 Jane Dutton and Amy Wrzesniewski, "What Job Crafting Looks Like," *Harvard Business Review*, March 12, 2020, www.hbr.org/2020/03/what-job-crafting-looks-like.

54 Katie Gilbert, "To Be Happier at Work, Think Flexibly about Your Job—and Yourself," Yale Insights, July 26, 2022, https://insights.som.yale.edu/insights/ to-be-happier-at-work-think-flexibly-about-your-job-and-yourself.

55 Jeffrey Ton, "Networking: It's Not What You Think," *Forbes Magazine*, October 15, 2020, www.forbes.com/councils/forbestechcouncil/2020/10/ 15/networking-its-not-what-you-think.

56 "Masterful Mentoring at Sun Microsystems," *Talent Management 360*, updated November 24, 2015, www.talentmanagement360.com/masterful-mentoring-at-sun-microsystems.

57 *Delivering Through Diversity*, McKinsey & Company, www.mckinsey.com/~ /media/mckinsey/business%20functions/people%20and%20organizational %20performance/our%20insights/delivering%20through%20diversity/ delivering-through-diversity_full-report.pdf.

58 Rocío Lorenzo, Nicole Voigt, Miki Tsusaka, Matt Krentz, and Katie Abouzahr, "How Diverse Leadership Teams Boost Innovation," *Boston Consulting Group*, January 23, 2018, www.bcg.com/publications/2018/how-diverse-leadership-teams-boost-innovation.

59 Oscar Trimboli, *How to Listen* (Vancouver: Page Two, 2020).

60 Robert Sutton and Ben Wigert, "More Harm Than Good: The Truth

About Performance Reviews," *Gallup.com*, May 6, 2019, www.gallup.com/workplace/249332/harm-good-truth-performance-reviews.aspx.

61 Jack Zenger and Joseph Folkman, "The Ideal Praise-to-Criticism Ratio," *HarvardBusinessReview.com*, March 15, 2013, www.hbr.org/2013/03/the-ideal-praise-to-criticism.

62 "Q&A With Malcolm Gladwell: 'Revenge of the Tipping Point,'" *David Epstein (Substack)*, October 1, 2024, www.davidepstein.substack.com/p/q-and-a-with-malcolm-gladwell-revenge.

ABOUT
THE AUTHOR

A LIFELONG GENERALIST, LEARNER, MAKER, and out-of-the-box thinker, Siobhán O'Riordan has always been curious about the connections between ideas, people, and possibility. She founded Big Sea Strategies to support clients navigating change, creating the space for connection and trust that fosters growth and impact.

A Gallup®-Certified CliftonStrengths® Coach and advisor, Siobhán has worked with hundreds of entrepreneurs, leaders, teams, new managers, and board members in over 100 organizations, with revenues ranging from $500,000 to $30 million. She has assisted in hiring talent, creating learning cultures, building a sense of belonging within workplaces, growing revenue, improving communications and collaborations, and developing capacity, strategies, programs, funding models, and messaging. Her work has been formally recognized, with awards from the *Boston Business Journal* (40 Under 40) and a New Ventures in Philanthropy Fellowship.

Siobhán's favorite role was teaching history at Lincoln School in Kathmandu, Nepal, where her love of learning, history, creativity, nature, and brain science found new meaning. Siobhán has a BA in History and an MA in Teaching, both from Tufts University, and lives in Massachusetts when she's not exploring the world near and far.